人人有功練

古語有云：「有功夫，無懦夫。」「一膽二力三功夫。」「只要功夫深，鐵杵磨成針。」「踏破鐵鞋無覓處，得來全不費功夫。」

已故偉大武術家李小龍曾說：「功夫如水，既是天底下至柔之物，卻能馳騁天下之至堅。水無形，故抓之不得，擊之無傷。」

康城影帝梁朝偉扮演的詠春宗師葉問說過：「『功夫』兩個字，一橫一直，錯嘅瞓低，企得番喺度會。」「『功夫』兩個字，係咪咁話？」

關於「功夫」二字的定義，真可謂各自表述，各自精彩。然則功夫到底為何物？在此分享幾則武林奇聞，或許會令諸位看官對「功夫」二字有另一種了解也未可知。

江湖傳聞，西方曾有一俊美電腦工程師，某天偶遇高人，有緣一窺宇宙實相，得悉自己一直活於虛擬世界，世間一切皆為幻相。後明查暗訪各門各派高手的武林軼事，並以畫作記錄，意圖通過繪畫過程領悟武藝之真義。然而天下沒有白吃的午餐，幾年下來，顧氏不但沒有練得一招半式，手臂更因長之間悉數學懂，教一眾武林高手嘖嘖稱奇。

在遙遠的東方，相傳南方某城市曾有一孩童，某日從路邊流浪漢手中購入《如來神掌》連環圖，每天依照書中記載的圖畫亂練時間作畫而筋疲力竭，一身病痛，後來有好心人不忍心顧氏白費功夫，通過現代印刷技術把畫作印製成書本廣為流傳，希望有緣遇上骨骼精奇的讀者，閱讀後能得到開示，成為打遍天下無敵手的高手。

正是：「人人有功練，有燈就有人。」

虛擬世界，世間一切皆為幻相。後明查暗訪各門各派高手的武林軼事，並以畫作記錄，意圖通過繪畫過程領悟武藝之真義。然而天下沒有白吃的午餐，幾年下來，顧氏不但沒有練得一招半式，手臂更因長之間悉數學懂，教一眾武林高手嘖嘖稱奇。

南方有一畫家顧氏，平時吊兒郎當，不務正業，大半時間沉迷於連環圖和東西方影畫戲。某日聞極無聊，竟妄想效法上述兩則江湖奇事的主人翁，通過影像之吸收於短時間內練成一身好武功。於是廢寢忘餐地觀看種種武功招式之出處，走遍大江南北追查種種武功招式之出處，一通，毫無長進。長大後卻因緣際會，弄假成真，練成了力量足可開山劈石的如來神掌。

"Everybody is Kung Fu Fighting"

The word "Kung Fu" exists in many ancient Chinese proverbs, with one of the most notable ones being: "Nobody's a coward when they learn Kung Fu". The late Kung Fu legend Bruce Lee also once said, "Kung Fu is like water, the world's softest substance that is also strong enough to penetrate rock and granite; water is also insubstantial, as one cannot grasp or punch to hurt it." Cannes film star Tony Leung, who played Ip Man in "The Grandmaster" (2013) concurred: "Two words, Kung Fu — two sides of light and dark, but the one left standing is the righteous one..."

This begs the question: what exactly is Kung Fu? The following few anecdotes may reveal an answer.

Legend has it that there was a handsome computer engineer from the West who, one fateful day, realised he was living in a simulated world under the control of a powerful man who wore sunglasses. After a period of intense training under said man, the engineer was able to download martial arts moves from various schools using the power of Western technology. Where others took decades, this Chosen One was able to replicate and master the moves in the blink of an eye, drawing the attention and amazement of other masters from around the globe.

On another fateful day in the Far East, there was a young boy who bought an ancient manual off an old homeless beggar. Although he practised the techniques day and night to no avail, a dormant power was awakened in him when his body was pushed to its limits years later, miraculously bestowing upon this Chosen One the strength to split mountains and crush rocks with the Buddha's Palm.

In the South, an artist named Koo was known for his dilly-dallying and slovenly tendencies, as well as his obsession with Kung Fu flicks and comics. One fateful day, he decided to imitate the two Chosen Ones mentioned above by absorbing the essence of Kung Fu through images alone. As a result, he spent day after day consuming Kung Fu films and even travelled across lands in an attempt to trace the origins of each martial arts technique to chronicle them through art. However, as they say, "there is no such thing as a free lunch", which is why his endeavours left him with next to nothing in terms of Kung Fu skills. To make matters worse, Koo also suffered from various ailments, having overexerted his arm from too much "art-ing". Fortunately, his work was noticed by kind-hearted folks who could not bear to see his efforts go to waste and circulated his work around the globe through the power of the printing press. Koo hopes that this book will fall into the hands of another Chosen One who will become enlightened and transform into the ultimate Kung Fu master.

That is to say, anyone can become a master as long as they are "Kung Fu Fighting"!

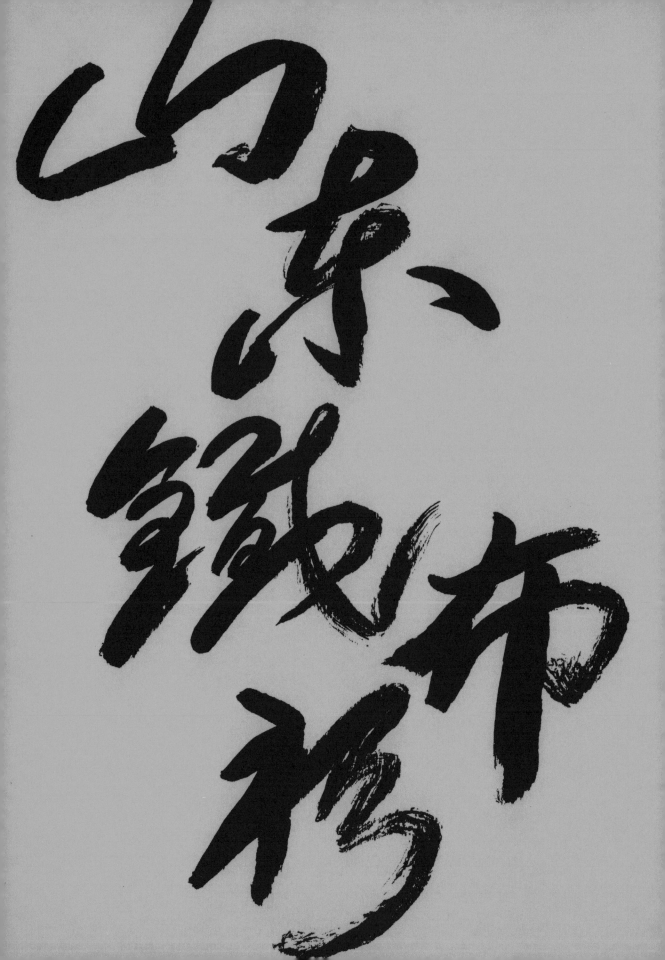

SHANDONG IRON VEST

山東鐵布衫

一種內外功兼修的功夫，練成後可抵擋拳腳兵刃，如穿上一層甲冑，與金鐘罩相類。有傳山東人喜練鐵布衫，山西人則對金鐘罩情有獨鍾，故武林有「東鐵布，西金鐘」之說。鐵布衫最早可追朔至清朝，作家蒲松齡創作《聊齋誌異》卷六〈鐵布衫法〉記載：一名姓沙的回民自稱懂得鐵布衫，不但能把五指併攏化為利刃，砍斷牛脖子，把牛肚子捅穿，甚至把自己的命根子掏出來，放在石頭上，拿木槌子使勁砸，也沒有一點損傷。故鐵布衫是許多男子爭相修練的奇妙神功。

江湖傳聞，山東武術界出過一位姓嚴名振東的武夫，精通鐵布衫。他於江湖寂寂無名，生活潦倒，一心想憑鐵布衫打出一片天。為了揚名立萬而往佛山，挑戰「廣東十虎」之一的黃飛鴻，卻遭拒絕。後來輾轉和黃飛鴻有過兩場比武，憑藉鐵布衫功夫一度和黃飛鴻鬥得難分難解，最後雖然不敵黃飛鴻，二人卻不打不相識，互相欽敬。聞說嚴振東後來身中洋人炮槍而亡，一代鐵布衫的大弟子梁寬曾拜嚴振東為師，卻沒有學過鐵布衫。山東鐵布衫從此失傳。

Shandong Iron Vest

The Shandong Iron Vest is a type of Kung Fu that utilises both the body and the spirit – one so strong, it can be used to resist all manner of punches and stabs like a layer of armour. Just as the Golden Shield was favoured in Shanxi, the Shandong people were avid practitioners of this technique, giving rise to the motto: "Iron Vest in the East, Golden Bell in the West". Its history traces all the back to the Qing dynasty, in particular, the book "Strange Tales from a Liaozhai" by famed writer Pu Songling. Not only could practitioners turn their fingers into sharp blades – even their nether regions could miraculously survive devastating hits. Unsurprisingly, it became widely sought-after by young men for its sheer, unbelievable power.

There was once a martial artist from Shandong known as Iron Robe or Yim Chun-Tung, who was relatively unknown in the local martial arts circle. To make a name for himself, he headed for Foshan – the capital of Chinese Kung Fu – to challenge Wong Fei-Hung, one of the Ten Tigers of Guangdong. Although he was rejected at first, Iron Robe eventually managed to showcase his skills in two future bouts with the legend himself, winning the latter's respect in both. Foon, Wong's eldest disciple, would end up training under Iron Robe for a time, but the technique was never passed on. When Iron Robe was shot dead years later, the "Iron Vest of the East" sadly became another artform forever lost to Western gunpowder.

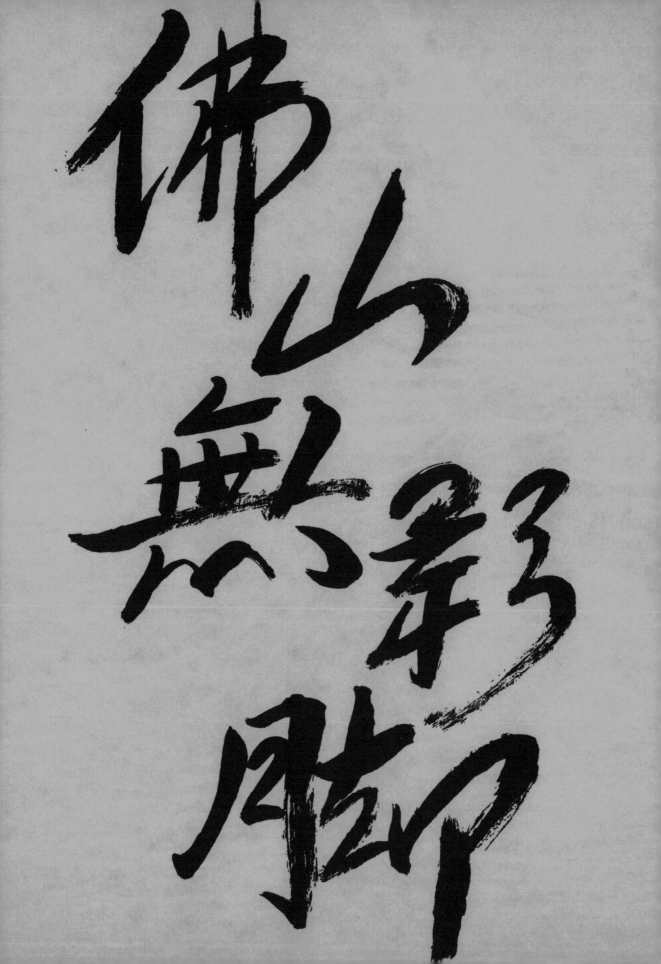

佛山無影腳

FOSHAN SHADOWLESS KICK

相傳西方有一種名為「多重宇宙」的現象，即一個人的作為會因應不同選擇而出現多種可能，而各種可能皆同時存在於日月星辰之間。外號「廣東十虎」之一的黃飛鴻，其事跡於江湖上亦有不少版本：高矮肥瘦、正氣猥瑣、嚴肅詼諧……甚至有黃飛鴻跟花旗國原住民出生入死，有黃飛鴻跟孫中山討論醫學，也有黃飛鴻作公雞打扮搗破邪教，正是：「一樣米養百樣人，百朵桃花一樹生。」

關於他的得意功夫佛山無影腳，亦有多個版本。有說南方拳種以手、腰為主，忽略了腳下功夫，而黃飛鴻則把北方的腿法套路融入南方拳裏面。無影腳強調腳法，腳下沉穩之餘，也能以快制敵。也有說出招時先以拳使出快招，讓人眼花繚亂，待其注意力被上盤吸引，再忽然起腳攻其下盤，是聲東擊西的戰法，在武術上並不算獨門絕技。亦有說無影腳即是「裙裡腳」，為女子穿着長裙，遮掩出腳動作的武術，神出鬼沒，難以提防。最匪夷所思的說法是要先跳起至三丈高，落下時雙腳向敵人連環踢擊，完全違反地心吸力。然而這卻是坊間最多人目睹的場景。

Foshan Shadowless Kick

In the Far West, there is a certain theory revolving around "the multiverse", where one's actions result in a plethora of hypothetic possibilities that exist all at once beyond our observable universe. Similarly, there are multiple discrepancies in the story of famed martial artist Wong Fei-Hung's past. Depending on the tale, the man also known as one of the Ten Tigers of Guangdong was tall, short, fat or thin. There were also multiple sides to his personality: righteous, wretched, serious, and witty all at once. Whether he fought alongside the Native Americans or enjoyed medical discourses with Sun Yat-Sen as various sources have claimed, the mystery surrounding his life has only multiplied over the years.

Even Wong Fei-Hung's trademark move, the Foshan Shadowless Kick, exists as multiple versions. Although boxing in the South – where he was from – placed greater emphasis on hand and waist movements, he made the technique all about footwork, incorporating leg movements from the North. Strong and steady, it could be performed at high speeds and paired with lightning-fast fistwork to distract and disarm the opponent. Some have even likened practising the Foshan Shadowless Kick to wearing a long skirt, as their lower-body attacks could be "obsured" through slick, unpredictable sequences. According to legend, one could harness the technique's full power by dealing a death-kick from as high up as 30 feet above the ground – a multiverse-shattering move, as it were.

FOUR WAY POLE

相傳由滿清提督納蘭元述所創，講究一氣呵成、剛勁勇猛、超強爆發。所謂的四門為四個方向之意，是以面對的單一方向，其上下左右的架隔分為四門。四門棍法要求練習者具備忠、勇、剛、毅等條件。納蘭元述後來在沖澡時得到靈感，以沾濕了水的布代替木棍，三尺白絹也能打出鋼筋鐵棒的力道。舞起來既有齊眉棍的剛猛，又有如軟鞭般的靈巧，是一套剛柔並濟的棍法。

且說「多重宇宙」裡其中一段黃飛鴻事跡。他應邀前往廣州，結識了革命家孫中山。當時有邪教白蓮教糾黨逞惡，借「扶清滅洋」口號妖言惑眾，搗亂使館、教堂等洋人地盤。原來白蓮教得到納蘭元述包庇，以對付革命黨。後來黃飛鴻隻身到白蓮教總壇搗亂，為救孫中山同黨，更於一窄巷內與納蘭元述作生死鬥。雖然納蘭元述以四門棍法與黃飛鴻鬥得不相伯仲，最後還是被黃飛鴻以竹竿割喉而死。也有說是納蘭元述打死了黃飛鴻，並追上孫中山及其同黨。卻原來孫中山也是武術行家，當場以一式日字衝拳了結納蘭元述，因此被後世尊稱「南拳北腿孫中山」。

Four Way Pole

Legend has it that the Four Way Pole was a technique created by Nalan Yuanshu, an admiral under the Qing dynasty. All about explosive power, the "Four Way" refers to the four directions that one's weapon should aim towards, as well as the four core virtues of loyalty, bravery, strength, and perseverance. As a form of training, Nalan Yuanshu was known to occasionally swap the pole for a wet towel, manifesting the strength of a reinforced iron rod and the dexterity of a whip through the piece of cloth.

In one of his multiverses, Wong Fei-Hung goes to Guangzhou at the invitation of the International Medical Association. There, he meets the revolutionary Sun Yat-Sen, who ends up being captured by members of a notorious, destructive cult called the White Lotus Sect. Eventually, it is revealed that the sect is under the protection of Nalan Yuanshu, leaving Wong with no choice but to find the sect's hideout and defeat the admiral to save Sun. Although the Four Way Pole is wielded against him, Wong emerges victorious by slitting Nalan Yuanshu's throat with a bamboo pole.

There is an alternate ending to this tale, where Nalan Yuanshu kills Wong Fei-Hung and catches up to a fleeing Sun Yat-Sen and his comrades. Lo and behold, Sun is revealed to be a great Kung Fu master himself and deals the death blow to the admiral, earning the title "Southern Fist Northern Kick Sun Yat-Sen".

SOARING KICK

沖天腳

一代武術宗師、「廣東十虎」之一的黃飛鴻曾於佛山設館授徒。傳聞他有一弟子劉七，外號「鬼腳七」，在拜師前曾於京城一帶拉人力車為生，所以體魄強健，閒時常自創武功，尤其喜歡鑽研下盤功夫，出腳快狠準，幾年下來已成高手。他生性莽撞，某日被不義之徒誘騙去廣東會館踢館，其時黃飛鴻之父黃麒英正在授教舞獅，大家一言不合，便打將起來。只見鬼腳七頭下腳上，以腳地大喝一聲：「沖天腳！」一隻腳猛地由下而上，把黃麒英踢飛至半空，重傷墮地。

但面對鬼腳七的攻勢也顯得左支右絀。鬼腳七倏代拳，不斷攻向黃麒英。黃麒英雖是洪拳名家，

由於鬼腳七肚裡沒半點墨水，所以從沒費心思為自創的腿法命名。那一句「沖天腳」也是一時興起，模仿連環圖的角色行為衝口而出，沒有半點美學考量。自從創出「沖天腳」，鬼腳七心癢難撓，開始正式為招式命名，甚麼「急急腳」、「前後腳」、「麻將腳」，一堆不知所云的破名字。後來他與黃氏一家冰釋前嫌，並拜黃飛鴻為師，性格變得開朗健談。鬼腳七身故後，他自創的招式名稱在廣東廣泛流傳，更演變成廣東俚語。

Soaring Kick

Wong Fei-Hung, one of the Ten Tigers of Guangdong, once ran a dojo for his disciples in Foshan – among whom was Kick Boxer or Liu Qi, a rickshaw puller in the capital. Due to his back-breaking work, he was extremely muscular and often spent time creating his own Kung Fu moves. Kick Boxer was also known to have a reckless temperament. Before joining the dojo, he was once lured by a shady character to cause a scene at the Cantonese Guild Hall where Wong's father, Wong Kei-Ying, was teaching the Lion Dance. A fight inevitably broke out between the two – and although the elder Wong was a master in the Hung Fist, he was no longer as sharp as he used to be and lost his footing, allowing Kick Boxer to drop-kick him with a "Soaring Kick!".

An illiterate coolie, Kick Boxer had never bothered to name his moves properly. Soaring Kick simply came to him in the heat of the moment, like the unpolished turn of phrase in a crude comic strip. After the hall incident, he thought long and hard about refining it – but Twinkle Toes and Mahjong Foot did not quite stick. Kick Boxer ended up training under Wong Fei-Hung out of respect for the latter's talent, becoming a bright, well-spoken man over time. However, his legendary Soaring Kick remained a popular colloquial expression long after his death.

ドラゴン
怒りの鉄拳
〈ブルース・リー作品〉

ブルース・リー
ノラ・ミャオ
ティエン・フォン
ボブ・ベイカー

怪鳥音が響きわたり！ ヌンチャクが唸る！

家

拳

糸

洪

泉铁

N WIRE FIST

洪家，即洪家拳，俗稱洪拳，屬南拳拳種，相傳已發展了三百多年，在廣東流傳甚廣。鐵線拳，少林外家拳之內功手法，是洪拳體系的代表拳術。鐵線拳之取義乃為剛柔兩用，蓋鐵為剛、線為柔，因此剛柔並濟，故名「鐵線拳」。以運動肢幹，暢通血脈為主。據聞具有壯魄健體，反弱為強的功能，恆久練習，有去病延年之效。

四十年代南方一帶，曾有一稱為城寨的貧民窟。城寨裡的居民表面上都是為錢銀奔波的老百姓，當中卻不乏身懷絕技卻已經隱退江湖的高手。由於年代久遠，許多傳聞已不可考證。但某些高手就像漆黑中的螢火蟲，永遠都如此出眾，被後世傳頌。聞說於江湖名震一時的鐵線拳高手趙師傅便曾經隱居其中，並化名裁縫勝在城寨內假裝裁縫，幹起替居民縫製藝術成分極高的華衣美服之行當。為了不使江湖同道起疑，甚至假裝娘娘腔，以掩飾起剛陽味。然而後來發生了一起打鬥事件，裁縫勝的真實身份還是暴露出來，最後甚至慘死於城寨裡。這場起源於黑幫與城寨居民間的衝突，演變成武林高手間的比拼，最後城寨建築甚至有一半被毀，史稱「城寨大毀滅」。

Hung Ga Iron Wire Fist

The Hung Ga Iron Wire Fist, commonly known as the Hung Fist, is a type of boxing technique from the South. With a history dating back to more than 300 years ago, its popularity has extended far and wide beyond its birthplace of Guangdong. The "Iron Wire" in its name stems from Shaolin techniques and is an iconic move that combines the rigidity of iron and the dexterity of wire: the hard and the soft. Thanks to its body-strengthening and blood vessel-unblocking properties, one could become strong, ward off sicknesses, and prolong their lifespan all at once through regular training.

In the 1940s, there was a Southern slum known as the Walled City, where ordinary folk seemed to live unremarkable lives on the surface. However, the city was in fact home to a good many retired masters of martial arts – revered to this day by future generations. Among them was Master Zhao, a famous wielder of the Hung Ga Iron Wire Fist. According to legend, he made beautiful clothes for residents under the alias Tailor Sheng, masking his true prowess under a meek and gentle demeanour to stay off the radar. Unfortunately, his real identity was revealed during a fateful brawl within the city walls that ended up killing him. The incident, which came to be known as the "Great Destruction of the Walled City", was said to have escalated from a petty conflict between residents and gangsters into a competition among the best martial artists in town.

路三

腿

TAN TUI TWELVE

二十

語 譚

ICKS TECHNIQUE

十二路譚腿

江湖上一直有「南拳北腿」的說法，「南拳」指的是洪拳，而「北腿」就是指譚腿，亦稱「潭腿」。傳說此腿法起源於山東龍潭寺，故稱為潭腿；還有一說由河南姓譚之人所創，故名譚腿；更有一說是由滄州姓譚名腿之人所創，故名譚腿。

愛因斯坦曾經講過：「練拳不練腿，如同冒失鬼。」傳說北方某城某鎮某男，姓甚名誰已不可考，家裡經營米店，為人嗜武，卻一直只練拳法而忽略了腿法馬步。說巧不巧，他的頭腦亦的確不太靈光，性格衝動，常擺烏龍。某日不知從哪裡讀到愛因斯坦那句名言，竟放棄家業，想也不想便去了嵩山少林學習譚腿，希望腿功精進的同時能改善頭腦。十年後學成下山，家人早已移居他鄉。某男傷心欲絕，輾轉流浪到南方，住進了城寨，取了個叫「咕哩強」（苦力）的外號，幹苦力維生。「結果我依然是一個莽夫，竟然用苦練的功夫來搬米！」他每晚都會為此自責，希望有天自己苦練的譚腿能派上用場。天從人願，後來發生的「城寨大毀滅」，起因正是由於咕哩強不忍居民被黑幫欺負，使出了譚腿對付，從而跟幾位高手引發了大型打鬥。聽說咕哩強當晚便被黑幫重金禮聘的高手暗殺，身首異處，死狀恐怖。

Tan Tui Twelve Kicks

In the world of Chinese Kung Fu, the motto "Southern Fist, Northern Kick" refers to a combination of the Hung Fist and Tan Tui or Tan Tui Twelve Kicks. Although some say the latter originated from the Longtan Temple, others believe that it was created by a man called Tan Tui, making it his namesake move.

The story goes that there was once an anonymous man from the North who was addicted to martial arts. In between boxing training, he would help his family out in their rice business. However, he was not the sharpest tool in the shed and often acted on impulse. He also tended to skip leg day; a big no-no even at the time. To make up for his lack of leg strength, he decided to hole up in the Shaolin mountains to work on the Tan Tui Twelve Kicks technique. After ten years in exile, he returned to his village – only to find that his family had moved away without him. Heartbroken but determined to make a new life for himself, he then relocated to the Walled City in the South and changed his name to Coolie Keung, making a living by carrying heavy loads. Each night, he would lament, "I've been a fool… Why am I using my hard-earned skills on hard labour instead of fights?" As if to grant his wish, a calamity befell the city, compelling Coolie Keung to use his skilful footwork against evil forces. Unfortunately, he was never to be seen again after the incident, having died a gruesome death in the hands of hitmen.

郎

棍

FIVE GUYS EIGHT

五
卦八
DIAGRAMS POLE

相傳由宋代楊家將之一的楊五郎始創。楊五郎隨父北征契丹，後到五台山出家為僧，因為佛門不可動刀槍，所以將長槍改成木棍，又將槍法變化成棍法。此棍法由太極生兩儀，兩儀生四象，四象生八卦，演變為六十四點棍法，符合內外八卦八八六十四之數，故名五郎八卦棍。

相傳隱居於城寨的高手中有一位是五郎八卦棍的大行家。他的真實姓名已不可考，只知道不懂粵語，會唸幾句不知所云的洋文，可能是來自北方的讀書人。某天他攜着幾根巨大的麵粉棍，自稱「油炸鬼」，就這樣住進了城寨，並在城內經營一家賣早點的小店。除了偶然會因欠租問題被包租婆責罵幾句，一直都跟居民相處融洽。直到後來發生了「城寨大毀滅」，油炸鬼忍不住出手相助，其武功才終於顯露出來。據居民憶述，油炸鬼某晚跟裁縫勝聯手，對付兩個同操一把古琴的二人組合。只見油炸鬼把麵粉棍舞得虎虎生風，最高風速能達每小時一百八十五公里，甚至令海面湧起暗浪。可惜最後不敵古琴二人組的琴音，命喪城寨。據包租公回憶，油炸鬼臨終遺言是一句洋文 "What are you prepared to do?" 其意義到現在還是一個謎。

Five Guys Eight Diagrams Pole

Legend has it that the Eight Diagrams Pole method was created by Yang Five Guy, a Song dynasty general from the Yang clan. A young Yang had followed his father on an expedition to Khitan one day, only to end up at a monastery in the Wutai mountains. As weapons were forbidden, he had to swap the spear he was carrying for a wooden stick. Over time, his stickwork – composed of 64 moves in eight diagrams – became the stuff of legend, giving rise to his namesake Five Guys Eight Diagrams Pole technique.

There was once a Kung Fu master living among the Walled City residents in the South who went under the nickname Donut. He did not speak a lick of Cantonese and was often mistaken to be a scholar from the North. Armed with a few dough sticks, Donut had simply appeared in the city one day and set up a small breakfast café that quickly became a local favourite. In the lead-up to the "Great Destruction of the Walled City", he and Tailor Sheng were pitted against a mysterious guzheng-playing duo who had appeared suddenly in the middle of the night. Witnesses purportedly saw Donut twirling two poles at a mindblowing speed of 185 km per hour, creating strong gusts of wind that made waves in oceans far away. Unfortunately, his skills proved to be no match for the powerful sound waves from the guzheng. According to the city's Landlord who was at the scene, Donut's last words sounded like, "What are you prepared to do?!" – but as they were uttered in a foreign tongue, what he actually meant to say remains a mystery.

式法琴

SIX MOVES ANTI

QUE PIANO SKILL

六式古琴法

此武功屬旁門左道，故多年來一直沒有一個正式名堂，有說是六式古琴法，有說是六式古箏法。相傳是以古箏彈奏樂曲，利用音波震碎對手五臟六腑，練至走火入魔的話，甚至能以魔音招魂，替其作惡。然而武林之大，無其不有，卻鮮少聽聞有高手領教過這套功法。

據城寨居民阿蓮憶述，「城寨大毀滅」前的某個深夜，大部份居民包括她早已熟睡。好夢正酣，阿蓮忽然被一股無以名狀的噪音吵醒，立刻往窗外張望，卻見中庭內坐着兩個衣着打扮一模一樣的男人，還戴着墨鏡，正肩並肩舞弄着一具古琴。在兩個怪人約五丈外站着兩位街坊，竟對着空氣舞拳弄棍。阿蓮再細看，發現兩位街坊對兩個怪人的樂曲似感到莫名難受，面露痛苦表情，身上不知何故出現越來越多傷口，眼見活不成了。就在此時，包租婆在自住的單位裡大喊一聲，震耳欲聾，中庭裡的四人立即停止了吵鬧，阿蓮也被那聲大喊震得昏了過去。後來聞說六式古琴法輾轉傳到西方，對一些西洋樂師產生了極大影響。聞說有一隊來自法蘭西的二人搭檔連打扮也受當年古琴二人組的影響呢！他們加以改良變奏後，形成所謂的電子舞曲。

Six Moves Antique Piano Skill

There is no official name for this martial art: some have deemed it the Six Moves Antique Piano Skill, while others continue to call it the Six Moves Guzheng Skill. Whichever name people know it by, it uses the sound waves produced by an antique piano or guzheng to shatter the opponent's internal organs. Players of the instrument who take their skills too far have even been known to become possessed by demons.

Ah Lian, a resident of the Walled City, was jolted awake one night by an indescribable noise coming from the courtyard below. Peering outside her window, her eyes came to focus on two sunglasses-clad kooks dressed in identical black garb. Standing side by side, they began playing a guzheng in harmony while facing off against two other residents. As the tune went on, Ah Lian noticed pained expressions beginning to form on the residents' faces, along with bloody gashes on their bodies. Eventually, they both fell to the ground – seemingly dead. Just then, the city's Landlady burst out of her flat and let out a deafening screech from her balcony, driving the kooks away.

At some point later on, the Six Moves Antique Piano Skill was brought to the West, where it caused a sensation among musicians. The technique was further tweaked to form a new genre of music called EDM, propagated by a certain French DJ pair who were said to be inspired by the Antique Piano Duo's sounds and style.

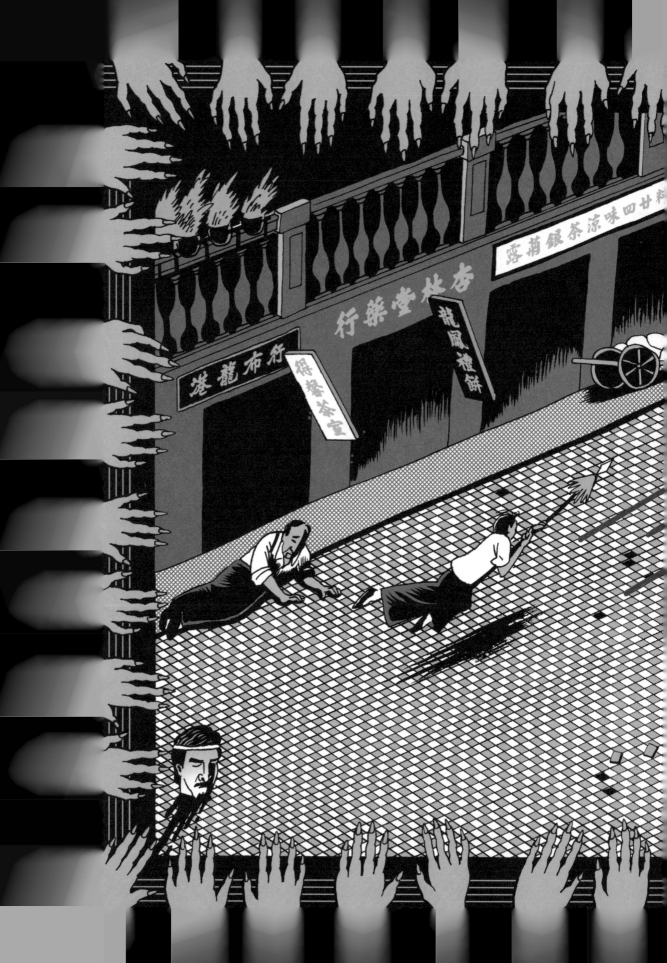

功隊

LION'S ROA

乱獅

R KUNG FU

又稱獅子吼，少林七十二絕技之一。此功為人體丹田內氣外發，發聲吐氣之功法，遇敵交手時發功呼嘯，猶如迅雷疾瀉傳出數里之外，令人肝膽俱裂，毛骨悚然，往往一聲長嘯便令對手倒地不起。江湖傳聞，世上有三個人是獅吼功的高手，其一是釋迦牟尼佛。據典籍記載，佛教中稱佛說法為獅子吼，以此來比喻如來法音猶如獅吼，降伏一切煩惱，震醒一切眾生顛倒夢想。其二是元朝末年，明教四大護法之一的金毛獅王謝遜，當年在王盤山試刀大會，只以一招獅子吼便收拾了與會群雄。其三則是神鵰俠侶的小龍女。

相傳楊過與小龍女隱退江湖後，並沒有疏於練武，某天竟練成了《九陰真經》記載的長生之術。時移世易，兩人經歷了數次朝代更替，由北方移徙至南方一個叫城寨的小社區。這時的楊過已人面全非，變成一個形貌猥瑣的好色大叔；小龍女更不堪，變成一個煙不離口的矮胖婦人。兩人靠着幾百年的積蓄，在城寨收購了幾個單位收租度日。由於城寨居民欠租問題非常嚴重，小龍女常與租客口角，加上本身有功夫底子，竟在不知不覺間練成了獅吼功。有傳楊過的斷臂後來重新長了出來，也是給小龍女的獅子吼罵出來的。

Lion's Roar Kung Fu

Also known as the Roaring Lion, the Lion's Roar Kung Fu is one of the 72 Arts of Shaolin. When exhaling "qi" or the vital force from the "dantian" or energy centre of the body, the practitioner's roar can take the form of a thunderstorm spreading out for miles. A single howl can even send shivers up and down opponents' spines, making them drop like pins.

There are only three people in the world who have mastered the Lion's Roar Kung Fu. The first being the Shakyamuni Buddha, who compared it to the sound of the Tathagata; the second being Jason, a golden-haired "lion king" from the Yuan dynasty; and the third being Xiao Long Nu, the beloved warrior from the Legend of Condor Heroes. After Xiao Long Nu and her husband Yang Guo retired from the fighting scene, they continued to train together in hopes of becoming immortal. At some point in time, the couple migrated to the Walled City in the South and ended up settling there for centuries. Originally a young stud, Yang Guo aged into a perverted old man who was completely out of shape. Xiao Long Nu also became unrecognisable – her fading beauty attributed to the pack of cigarettes she would smoke each day. With their centuries' worth of savings, the couple eventually became the Landlord and Landlady of the slum. Due to her frequent squabbles with tenants, Xiao Long Nu mastered the Lion's Roar Kung Fu over time – her skillset so deafeningly powerful that it caused Yang Guo's once-severed arm to grow whole again.

吸
EXHALE

呼
INHALE

呼

INHALE

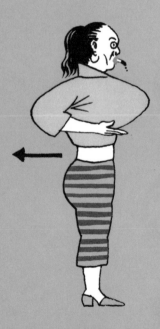

吸

EXHALE

拳椿

TAI CH

極大

FIST

世界級非物質文化遺產，以中國傳統儒道哲學中的太極、陰陽辯證理念為核心思想，集頤養性情、強身健體、技擊對抗等功能為一體。動作看似緩慢，但永不停頓。在太極拳中，速度並不是最重要的事，要旨是永遠保持平衡和穩定。

古時浙江一帶有一著名說書人「海寧查氏」，曾鉅細無遺地記錄了武林高手楊過前半生的遭遇，然而卻隻字未提楊過懂得太極拳。連查氏也不知道，楊過當初在全真教曾偷看過太極拳譜，只是後來奇遇連連，不斷有高人指點武功，太極拳就這樣擱了下來。後來楊過跟小龍女重遇，並一起練成了《九陰真經》記載的長生之術。古語有曰：「變色感情誰人留得住，再等痴情回流殊不易。」幾百年的朝夕相對，二人的感情終歸逃不過日漸變淡的宿命。後來因為政見不同，甚至開始打罵起來。雖然楊過每次都選擇默默承受小龍女的美女拳法，然而二人武功旗鼓相當，多年捱打的結果終於引致身體內傷，筋骨移位。楊過痛定思痛，決定修練太極拳的「四兩撥千斤」，以承受小龍女的攻擊。果然，一個願打一個願挨，夫婦二人的感情從此得以維繫。正是：「一夜夫妻百日恩，床頭打交床尾和。」

Tai Chi Fist

Based on Confucianism, Taoism, and the dialectical concepts of Yin-Yang, Tai Chi integrates elements like self-cultivation, physical fitness, and combat into a single artform, making it an invaluable cultural heritage. While its movements are slow, there is not a moment of pause in between. In Tai Chi, balance and stability always triumph over speed.

In ancient times, a storyteller named Cha from Haining became famous for chronicling the life of Yang Guo, a Tai Chi Fist master. However, not a single word was ever mentioned about how the latter gained knowledge of the technique. It eventually came to light that Yang Guo had secretly snuck a peek at a Tai Chi Fist manual at the Quanzhen School, where he perfected his craft with the help of other masters.

After meeting his future wife Xiao Long Nu, Yang Guo began practising the technique for attaining immortality as recorded in the Nine Shadow Scriptures. Although they eventually became immortal together as the Landlord and Landlady of the Walled City, the couple were not immune to the inevitable fading of romance. Over time, they began drifting further apart, fighting with each other at the slightest of provocations. To counter Xiao Long Nu's increasingly brutal attacks, Yang Guo took to practising the Tai Chi Fist again – in hopes of restoring his often-bruised body. Like Yin and Yang, they proved that a relationship could last through the ages even if they were polar opposites.

功蟻

MAGIC POW

莫蛤

ER OF TOAD

屬陽剛硬功，發功時蹲在地下，雙手彎與肩齊，嘴裡發出咯咯叫聲，宛似大青蛙作勢相撲，威力十足。要旨在於以靜制動，全身蓄勁涵勢，只要敵人一攻擊，立時便以猛烈無比的勁道反擊。相傳為西域奇人歐陽鋒所創，說書人海寧查氏於《射鳥英雄傳》有詳細記載。據聞蛤蟆功失傳多時，最後一次有人見到武夫演示已是四十年代。

話說小龍女以獅吼功擊退古琴二人組後，黑幫頭目找來因練功走火入魔而住進精神病院的火雲邪神與楊過夫婦對戰。火雲邪神來歷不明，沒有門派與徒弟，師承何處也是個謎。他不單是蛤蟆功高手，傳聞甚至能徒手接下西洋槍炮發射的鋼珠。

且說一輪苦戰後，楊過夫婦眼見勝券在握，最終卻遭火雲邪神使詐暗算。數天後，有城寨居民目擊火雲邪神跟一名白衣人毆鬥，並一度使出蛤蟆功。只見其身體脹大一倍有餘，四肢撐開，眼部突出，喉間不斷發出怪音，模樣驚人，撐腿一躍便是幾丈高。後來官府派人作官方調查，發現城寨有半數居民從此罹患一種對蛤蟆感到恐懼的心理病，有女居民甚至從此不敢到市場買菜做飯，以致不能料理家事而終生未嫁。由於發功時的模樣令人不安，傳說中的蛤蟆功從此失傳。

Magic Power of Toad

A tough technique to master, the Magic Power of Toad involves squatting on the ground with one's hands bent at shoulder-level while emitting a croaking sound – not unlike taking the stance of a sumo-wrestling frog. In unleashing its full power, the point of the technique is to store one's body full of energy before charging ferociously like an uncoiled spring as soon as the opponent attacks. According to the records of Cha, a storyteller from Haining, the Magic Power of Toad was created by a strange man from the West called Ouyang Feng.

Legend has it that after Xiao Long Nu used the Lion's Roar Kung Fu to defeat the Ancient Piano Duo, the latter's gang leader decided to hire the Beast, who had been institutionalised for brutally attacking Xiao and her husband Yang Guo during a previous bout. Although the origins of the Beast are unknown, he was a master in the Magic Power of Toad and could even catch bullets with his bare hands. A few days after the encounter between Xiao and the Duo, some residents of the Walled City witnessed the Beast fighting a man dressed in white. Not only had the former doubled in size with his out-stretched limbs, his eyes were also bulging as strange gurgles emanated from his throat. Using his terrifying physique, the Beast was able to jump several metres into the air in a single leap. After the incident, half of the residents were found to have developed an unhealthy fear of amphibians, causing the legendary Magic Power of Toad to fade into oblivion.

掌神

BUDDHA

來如

'S PALM

如來神掌

《紅樓夢》作者曹雪芹有句名言：「假作真時真亦假，無為有處有還無。」如來神掌既沒拳譜又沒心法，亦與如來佛祖毫無關係，相傳是由寶島說書人柳氏虛構的天佛掌演變而來，經多番改編，加上近代映畫戲的演繹和連環圖畫師黃氏的圖譜，構成了後世人們所認識的如來神掌。雖是虛構的武功，據聞還真有骨骼精奇、天賦異稟之士弄假成真，按照連環圖練成了如來神掌。

話說四十年代，有上海人周某，生性高傲但宅心仁厚。兒時曾依著《如來神掌》連環圖亂練一通，卻毫無成效。長大後成為專業墨七（小偷），有天走進城寨行騙不果，跟居民發生衝突，後來事情越演越烈，變成幾位早已隱退武林的高手較量，周氏更被黑幫殺手火雲邪神打至重傷。傷癒後的周氏意外被打通了任督二脈，兒時對如來神掌的記憶於體內分解再重組，竟就這樣學懂了如來神掌。脫胎換骨後的周某跟火雲邪神於城寨決戰，並以如來神掌擊敗火雲邪神。由於如來神掌的威力過於驚人，令幾乎大半的民居被毀，中庭亦留下一個半丈深的巨型掌印，史稱「城寨大毀滅」。因損毀嚴重，人們後來索性把城寨移為平地，並改建成高密度的富貴住宅和豪華市集。

Buddha's Palm

Cao Xueqin, the author of "Dream of the Red Chamber" once said, "Truth becomes fiction when the fiction becomes true; reality becomes unreal where the unreal becomes reality." This phrase applies to the Buddha's Palm, which strangely enough, has nothing to do with the Buddha. A storyteller from Formosa was said to have made up a story about the Heavenly Buddha Palm, which ended up being adapted into a film and a comic series. Although fictitious, a few Chosen Ones actually managed to master this technique.

In the 1940s, there was an arrogant but kind-hearted teenager called Zhou who grew up trying to master the Buddha's Palm – but to no avail. Instead, he became a thief who got swept into a Walled City conflict after an unsuccessful swindling attempt. While he was getting pummelled by the Beast, one of his veins was accidentally sliced open – causing fragments of the technique he learned long ago to become whole. Armed and transformed, Zhou successfully defeated his foe, but because his power was so overwhelming, he destroyed most of the dwellings in the vicinity, bringing about the "Great Destruction of the Walled City". Over time, what was left of the slum became luxury developments – making the Buddha's Palm a rich piece of history.

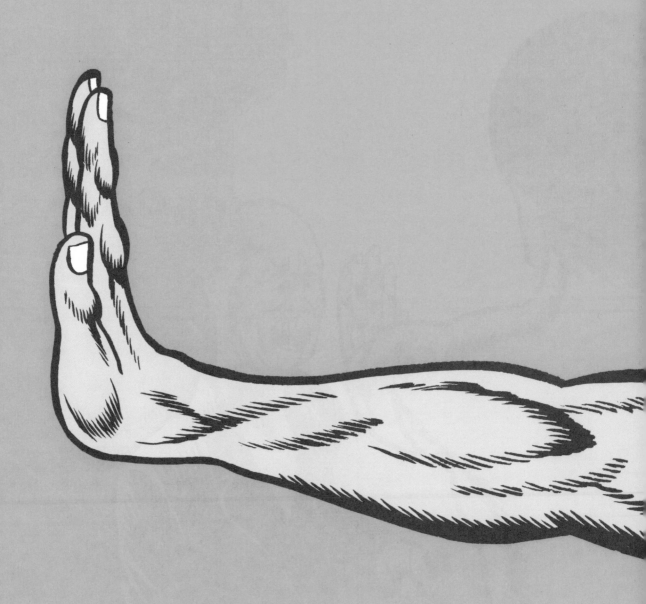

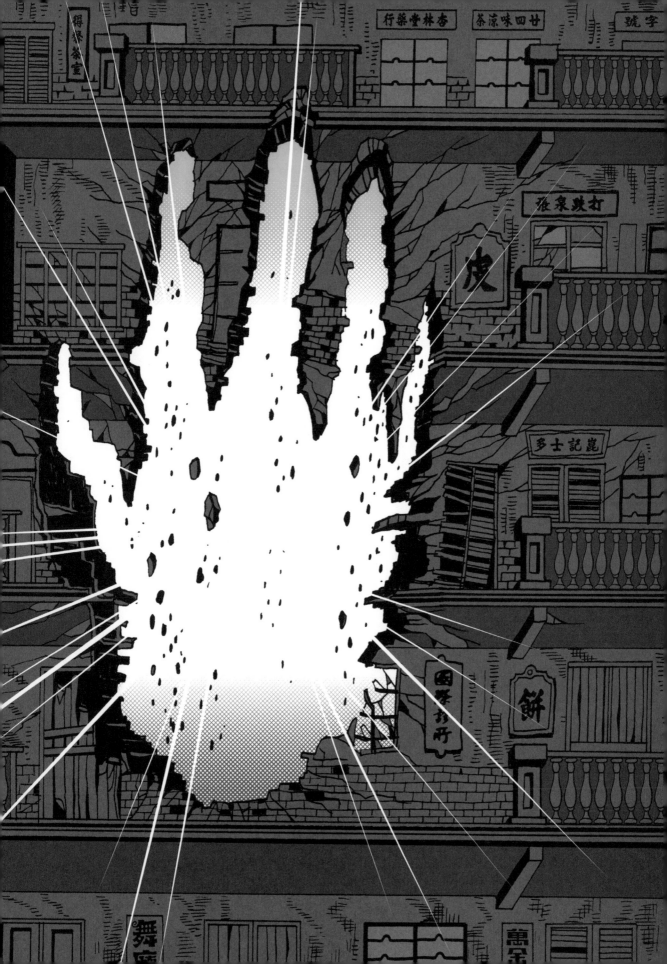

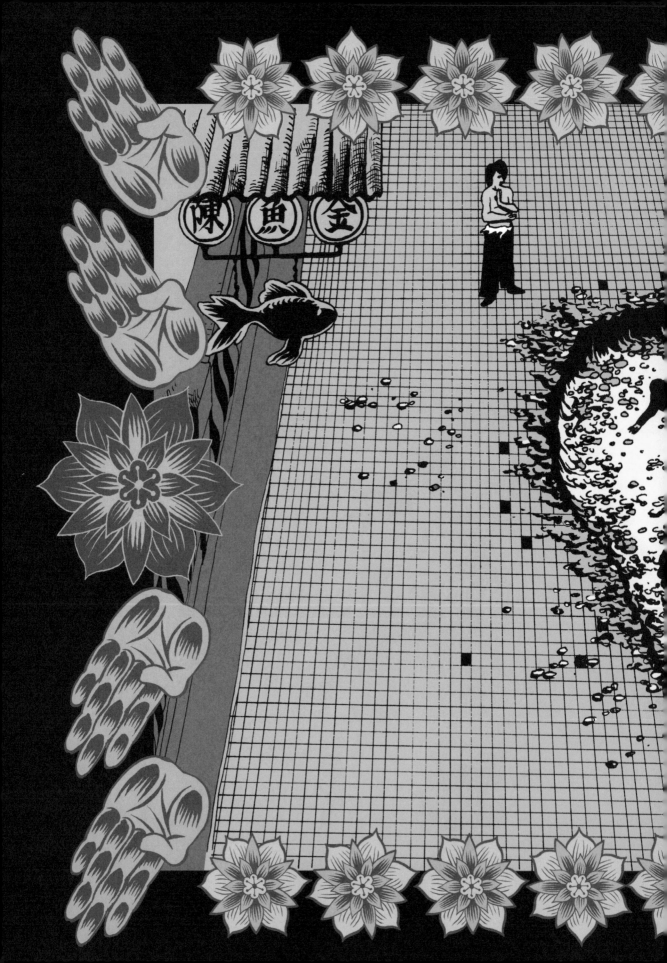

BRUCE LEE · JAMES TIEN · DAN INOSANTO · KAREEM ABDUL-JABBAR · HWANG IN-S

ALWAYS be YOURSELF, express YOURSELF, have FAITH in YOURSELF, do not go out and look for a successful personality an
Empty your mind, be FORMLESS. SHAPELESS, like WATER. You put water into a bottle and it becomes the bottle. You put it
Now, water can flow or it can crash. Be WATER, my friend.

BRUCE
LEE

GAME
OF
DEATH

K in **GAME OF DEATH**

licate it.
teapot, it becomes the teapot.

IRON HEAD
KUNG FU

鐵頭功

少林寺絕技之一，於實戰中以頭部撞擊對手，為硬氣功的一種，屬剛陽之勁。功力最深者觸石立碎，觸鐵板亦能深陷。修此功者，需藉由每日飲食中攝取含鈣質的食物來逐漸強化頭蓋骨的硬度。由於外物撞擊頭部有可能導致腦震盪，故修練此武功有一定危險性，輕則變成腦殘，重則吐血身亡。

話說上世紀中葉，少林寺有幾位武僧於少林三十六房修練不同武功。後來因學費每年上漲，眾人負擔不起，無奈一起下山各奔前程。大師兄到大城市謀職，信心滿滿地於履歷書「技能」一欄填上「鐵頭功」，卻被當成傻子轟出門，又不恥於街頭賣藝。好不容易在一間酒家找到清潔工作，因為工作態度原因，常被老闆用酒樽往頭上招呼。可幸大師兄從來沒有疏於練功，頭顱和工作尚能保得住。

某日，當年少林寺的五師弟忽然到訪。原來他悟出一種糅合傳統武術於球技的新型蹴鞠（足球）戰術。如果能把鐵頭功應用於頭槌上，一定能夠戰無不勝。後來大師兄經過一番內心掙扎，終於重拾初心，與其餘幾位師兄弟組成功夫蹴鞠團，從此把鐵頭功發揮得淋漓盡致，在蹴鞠場上大展所長，重振雄風。這也是少林寺著名的勵志故事。

Iron Head Kung Fu

One of the rarer Shaolin stunts, the Iron Head Kung Fu is a type of hard Qigong that involves using one's head to shatter stones and iron plates. Since blunt force trauma can cause life-threatening concussions, practitioners were known to harden their skulls through high calcium intakes: a habit that would safeguard them from risk factors such as cerebral incapacitation and death from blood loss.

In the middle of the last century, several monks were forced to leave the Shaolin Temple because training fees were getting too expensive. Upon applying for his first job in the big city, First Brother listed his main skillset as "Very Hard Iron Head" – only to be chased away for being a madman. Eventually, he found employment as a cleaner at a restaurant, where he was often greeted in the mornings with an empty glass bottle to the head. Fortunately, First Brother was a master of the Iron Head Kung Fu, which enabled him to protect his cranium and livelihood.

One day, First Brother received an unexpected visitor in the form of Fifth Brother, who was assembling a new soccer team that merged modern tactics with traditional martial arts. After some soul-searching, First Brother decided to leave his cleaning days behind him to join the team. By training and regaining his strength, he became a star on the field, headbutting his way into history.

WHIRLWIND
HOOKING LEG

相傳上世紀中葉，有少林武僧往西方取經，途經一西洋體能訓練學堂，窺見幾位弟子操練一種奇怪武功：雙腳張開成大字形，雙手支撐地，利用腰力令雙腿旋轉。上前查問何名堂，答曰：「湯馬斯迴旋。」武僧深受啟發，回少林寺後日夜苦練，並糅合山東地趟拳的跌撲滾翻動作，演變成旋風地堂腿，是一門中西合璧的腿法。

且說當年一起練武的幾位少林師兄弟，多年後下山還俗各奔前程。二師兄旋風地堂腿由於武功了得，竟頗受商賈垂青，爭相聘用。尤其需要電能生產的廠商，都因旋風地堂腿的旋轉力而大大提高了生產力。二師兄每逢周日又會到不同社福機構提供免費的風力發電。所謂「腎之華在髮」，幾年過去，由於長期的腰腿勞動，他開始腎虛脫髮。曾經濃密烏黑的一頭秀髮一下子所剩無幾，渾噩度日，最後淪落到幹二師兄不禁意志消沉，洗碗清潔之類的低下工作。可幸後來遇上五師弟，加入了功夫蹴鞠團，重新感受到旋轉的奧妙。相傳南北少林皆受二師兄的遭遇啟發，將鍛練旋風地堂腿的訓練場改建成旋風電力堂，為社會提供免費電力，造福人群。最妙的是：和尚沒有脫髮煩腦，大家高興。

Whirlwind Hooking Leg

Legend has it that a certain Shaolin monk was in the middle of a pilgrimage in the West when he happened to walk past a physical training school, where several disciples were practising a strange martial art that looked like the Thomas Flair. Deeply inspired by what he saw, the monk began practising the same move upon returning to the Shaolin Temple. He also devised a hybrid version of it, combining the Thomas Flair with fluttering movements from the Shandong Rolling Fist – thus giving rise to the Whirlwind Hooking Leg technique.

When training fees at the temple became too costly to bear, the Shaolin brothers were forced to go their separate ways. Second Brother's skillset ended up being favoured by merchants, in particular, manufacturers who needed electricity generated by the Whirlwind Hooking Leg. Over time, due to all the repetitive waist and leg movements, Second Brother began experiencing kidney and hair loss problems, eventually falling into a deep depression. Fortunately, he joined Fifth Brother's Shaolin soccer team, where he slowly found joy in practising the technique again. So inspiring was Second Brother's turnaround that even the Shaolin monastery transformed its inherently hair-free training grounds into a cyclone power generating facility, providing free electricity for society.

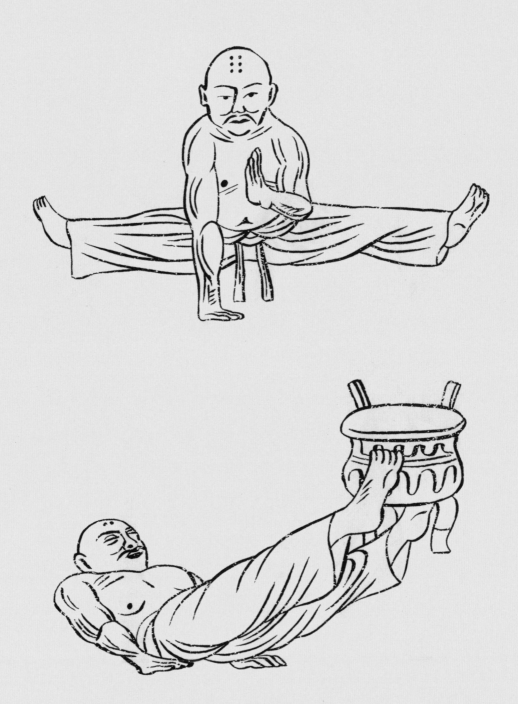

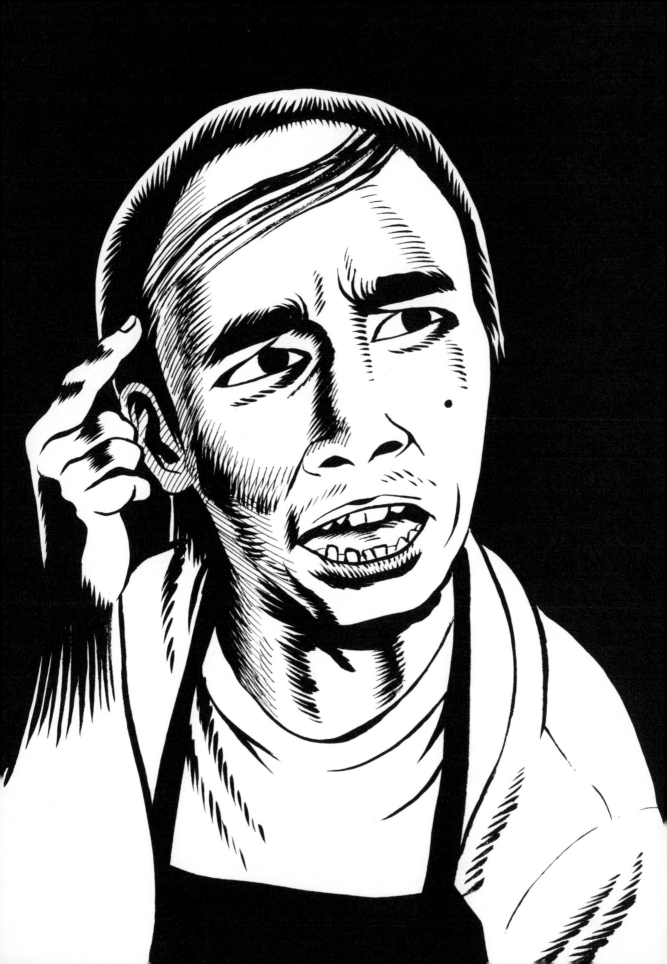

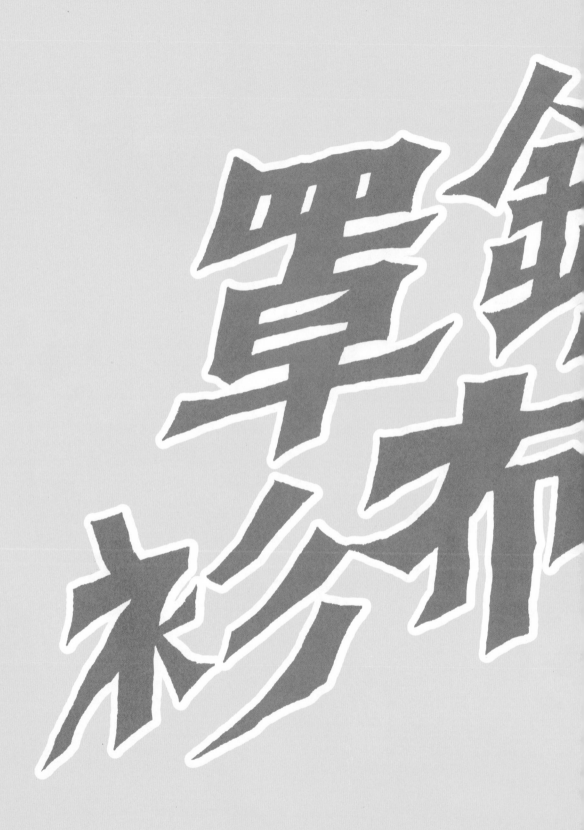

金鐘罩鐵布衫

金鐘罩鐵布衫是中國武學中知名的護體硬氣功，傳說練成的人不但可以承受拳打腳踢而絲毫無損，甚至能抵擋刀劍槍炮。事實上金鐘罩和鐵布衫是兩種不同的功法，可能因為金鐘罩和鐵布衫是個品牌之故，不少門派的護體硬氣功都叫這個名字，亦有不知就裡的人以為鐵布衫是指西洋避彈衣。

且說功夫蹴鞠團幾位同門師兄弟，大師兄練鐵頭功，二師兄修地堂腿，三師兄則練成了金鐘罩鐵布衫。後來各人落魄紅塵，相傳三師兄覺得金鐘罩的金字吉利，於是盲打誤撞進了金融業，過着每秒幾十萬兩銀升跌的數字人生，由一個曾經銅皮鐵骨的武僧變成市儈勢利的投機者。可幸後來遇上五師弟，與當年的師兄弟組成了功夫蹴鞠團，更於全國大賽以金鐘罩鐵布衫硬生生擋下了對方的攻勢，立下大功。

可惜好景不常，功夫蹴鞠團雖然憑武藝於全國大賽拿下了冠軍寶座，紅遍全國，但三師兄由於過分沉迷於名利帶來的快感，很快便退出球隊，變回一個投機主義者。後來據說因炒賣虛擬貨幣輸光了身家，於香江交易所頂樓蹤身一躍自盡。一代金鐘罩鐵布衫最終變成一堆廢鐵收場。

Golden Shield Iron Vest

The Golden Shield Iron Vest is a well-known hard Qigong in Chinese martial arts used to protect the body. According to legend, people who practise the technique can not only take punches and kicks without sustaining any damage, but also withstand sword attacks, piercing spears, and even gunshots. However, the Golden Shield Iron Vest is not to be confused with body armours or bullet-proof suits of the West.

In the Shaolin soccer team, First Brother was an expert in the Iron Head technique, whereas Second Brother was considered the master of the Whirlwind Hooking Leg. Third Brother, on the other hand, was a wielder of the Golden Shield Iron Vest who took the "gold" in its name as an auspicious sign to enter the financial trading industry after leaving the monastery. In a stroke of luck, he bumped into Fifth Brother and joined the team to reunite with his Shaolin brothers. During one of the championship matches, he forcibly blocked an opponent's offensive with his Golden Shield Iron Vest and helped his team secure a victory. Sadly, the good times did not last: although the team won the championship in the end, his martial arts skills became popular all over the country. Third Brother soon quit the team and became the money-chasing opportunist he once was. Later on, he was said to have thrown himself off the top floor of the Hong Kong Stock Exchange after losing his entire fortune in cryptocurrency – turning a generation of Golden Shields and Iron Vests into a pile of scrap metal.

PHANTOM
LITNING HAND

即擒拿手，鬼影二字純粹是命名者因美學考慮而強加上去，實情與鬼和影並無關係。擒拿屬於中國武術技法，源於技擊。利用人體關節、穴位和要害部位的弱點，運用槓桿原理與經絡學說，採用反關節動作和集中力量攻擊對方薄弱之處，使其產生無法抗拒的疼痛，達到擒其一處而擒之的效果。世界各地都有傳統或現代的擒拿術，並受到軍事單位的青睞，用以制服無辜百姓。

且說功夫蹴鞠團幾位同門師兄弟，個個皆精於一種武功，獨當一面。其中四師兄「擒拿手」不單武藝了得，相貌亦非一般，一張臉長得跟已故偉大武術家李小龍非常相似。正因如此，四師兄下山不久便受到戲行垂青，紛紛向他拋出表演機會，角色全都以模仿李小龍為主。廣告推銷、產品代言、直播帶貨、二流功夫片、庸俗電視劇，四師兄一下子變成搶手貨，忙得不可開交。不久後，江湖上開始出現各種「抄襲」、「剽竊」、「假致敬真搵銀」的指責，四師兄受不住群眾壓力，毅然退出戲行，決定在家「躺平」。後來得五師弟熱心相助，負責功夫蹴鞠團的龍門位置，鬼影擒拿手才得以派上用場。據聞四師兄從此絕跡戲行，卻不代表李小龍的模仿者自此消失。

Phantom Lightning Hand

At some point or other, close combat techniques have been used by military units around the world to subdue both enemies and innocent civilians. At its core a grappling movement, the phrase "Phantom Lightning" was only added to the name of this Chinese martial art to increase its appeal. Based on meridian theory, the Phantom Lightning Hand uses counter-joint movements and concentrated force to attack the opponent's joints, acupoints, and vital parts. As a consequence, the victim experiences excruciating pain and can be easily captured.

Each member of the Shaolin soccer team was talented in their own right: Fourth Brother or Lightning Hands not only excelled in martial arts, but also had a handsome face that resembled the late Bruce Lee. Because of this, he was offered numerous performance opportunities by casting agents – all of them as a Bruce Lee impersonator. From advertisements, product endorsements and live broadcasts to second-rate Kung Fu movies and TV dramas, Fourth Brother eventually became a film sensation. However, accusations of plagiarism, false tributes, and identity theft began to flood in, forcing him to fade out of the scene due to the pressure. It was only after Fifth Brother reached out to him that Lightning Hands returned to the limelight once more as the goalie of the Shaolin soccer team. Although Fourth Brother never acted again, he inspired a host of Bruce Lee imitators who remain popular in the industry to this day.

輕水

WATER WALK
SUBTLE STEPS

輕功水上飄

「水上飄」出自宋朝時期江南大幫派鐵掌幫幫主裘千仞的外號「鐵掌水上飄」，是命名者為增添詩意而強加上去的。輕功是中國傳統武術中真實存在的功法，雖不能使人的體重變輕，卻可大幅提高其奔跑和跳躍的能力，令人站立或行動於不可承重的物體之上，甚至提氣借用輕盈小物體騰起於空中。不需要奔跑鼓勢，只需兩足一蹬，即可起高躍遠，其起如飛燕掠空，其落如蜻蜓點水，落地無聲。是盜賊和懦夫的練武首選。

且說功夫蹴鞠團幾位少林同門師兄弟，因學費每年上漲而決定還俗。六師弟「輕功水上飄」因頭腦蠢笨，下山近一年後才找到工作，都是些低技術、不需動腦筋和體力勞動的行業。由於好吃懶做，不過幾個月時間，他便由面如冠玉的瘦削小生變成一塊既肥且膩的五花腩肉。加上下山後疏於練習，幾乎把輕功忘得一乾二淨。六師弟的存在彷彿只為了證明世上還有地心吸力。後來經五師弟拉攏，加入了功夫蹴鞠團，六師弟才重新憶起輕如無物的快感。踢過幾場球賽後，六師弟還是退出了蹴鞠團。據聞他後來從事餐飲快遞行業，憑着一身輕功，又受惠於疫症大流行期間老百姓多了送餐需求，因此賺了個盆滿缽滿。

Water Walk Subtle Steps

The term "Water Walk" is said to come from the nickname of Qiu Qianren or Iron Palm Water Walk, who was the leader of the Iron Palm Gang from the Song dynasty. Contrary to what people think, although Qinggong is a proper training technique in traditional Chinese martial arts, it does not make one's bodyweight lighter. Instead, it significantly improves their ability to run and jump, even on the lightest objects. With one kick, the practitioner can rise as high up as a swallow and leap far distances, landing lightly like a dragonfly on water. This made Water Walk Subtle Steps the martial art of choice for thieves and cowards.

Upon returning to the secular world due to the increase in training fees, Sixth Brother or Light Weight was the last to be employed among his brothers from the Shaolin Temple. Due to his slow wit and lazy nature, he went from having a thin and lanky physique to an overweight and greasy one in just a few months, with gravity being his only friend. He had almost forgotten his Qinggong training entirely – until Fifth Brother persuaded him to join the Shaolin soccer team. Thereafter, he began to enjoy being Light Weight again.

Legend has it that Sixth Brother finally quit the soccer team to join the food delivery industry. During the pandemic, he greatly benefitted from the increased demand, making a killing of a different kind with his nimble footwork.

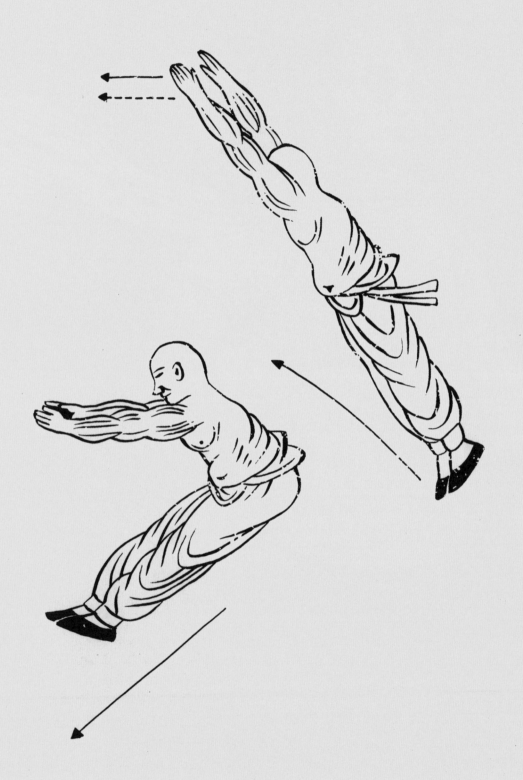

MIGHTY
STEEL LEG

即少林金剛腿，是少林鷹派拳術金剛功法之八。武林中歷來有「南拳北腿」之說，少林金剛腿就是北腿之一。武諺有云：「手是兩扇門，全憑腿打人。」充分說明腿法在技擊格鬥中的重要。少林金剛腿實而不華、靈活機動、凌厲威猛，在實戰中，時而硬打硬進；時而避敵鋒芒；時而出其不意，攻其不備；時而含而不露，誘敵深入。

且說功夫蹴鞠團幾位同門師兄弟下山後落魄紅塵。五師弟「金剛腿」生性高傲，不恥於江湖賣藝，又不屑於幹投機買賣的營生，而且對大地主的壟斷行為十分反感。他下山後靠拾荒為生，並於某大地主的大型市集上建了一座小茅屋棲身，算是對不公平社會的小小反抗。他做人不忘本，儘管生活潦倒，仍熱心推廣少林武功。某天偶遇外號「黃金右腳」的前足球名將，聞話幾句後深受啟發，決定糅合傳統武術於球技當中，並找來當年的師兄弟組成功夫蹴鞠團，最後憑少林武功於全國大賽拿下冠軍。後來五師弟與賣饅頭的太極高手小梅致力把傳統武術應用於不同運動，如羽毛球、桌球等，甚至把少林三十六房的武功鑄成非同質化代幣（NFT），開發元宇宙，把少林武功引進虛擬世界，史稱「人人有功練」。

Mighty Steel Leg

The Mighty Steel Leg or Shaolin Steel Leg is the eighth move in Shaolin Eagle Boxing and is one of the Northern kicks referred to in the motto: "Southern Fist, Northern Kick". It is also a testament to the importance of legwork, based on a popular maxim in Wuyan that goes: "Your hands are two doors; hit with your legs only." Solid but subtle, flexible but powerful, the Mighty Steel Leg can be used to not only attack an opponent with brute force, but also avoid counter-attacks, allowing the practitioner to lure, strike, and kill.

Fifth Brother or Mighty Steel Leg was known to be arrogant in nature and would bust his Kung Fu moves at any opportunity. However, he was also repulsed by speculative trading and unscrupulous landlords. After leaving the Shaolin Temple, he scavenged for a living and made his home in a thatched hut as a small act of resistance, never once forgetting his roots. One day, he was convinced by a former football star to join a unique genre-bending soccer team where he could showcase his skillset. Together with his brothers from the monastery, Fifth Brother ended up winning the national championship. Later on, he met a steamed bun-selling Tai Chi master called Mui, with whom he began combining traditional martial arts with different types of sports around the world, such as badminton, billiards, and shuttlecock kicking. The duo even minted NFTs of all 36 Shaolin Kung Fu moves, introducing a classic artform into the modern metaverse.

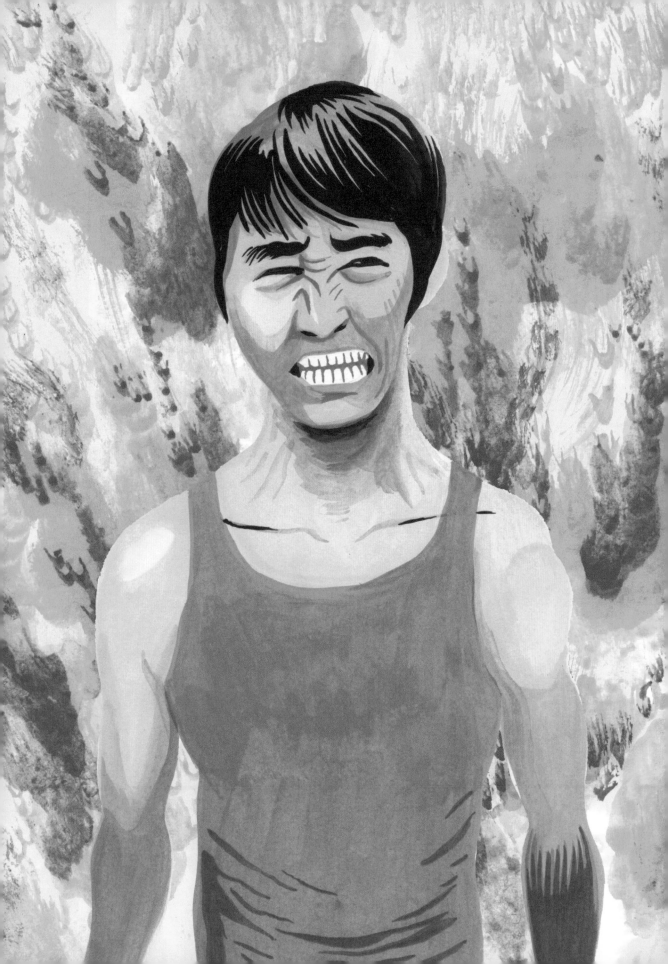

TAI CHI
UNLOADING FORCE

太極四両撥千斤

阿基米德曾說過：「給我一個支點，我就能撬起地球。」從物理角度分析，四両撥千斤就是利用了槓桿原理。而從武術技法理解，則是一種術語。太極拳《打手歌》：「任他巨力來打我，牽動四両撥千斤」，意謂順勢借力，以柔制剛。凡加引化勁於對手動作上，誘其落空；或者以橫撥直，卸開對方勁力等，均屬四両撥千斤之法。

相傳上世紀南方某村鎮，曾有一賣饅頭的太極拳高手小梅。她臉上長滿麻子，一雙眸子卻燦若繁星。她賣的饅頭以煙韌、細緻、綿密而知名，原因就是她以太極手法搓麵粉，所以蒸出來的饅頭剛中有柔、柔中有剛，口感變化多端。食客都大讚，吃過小梅的饅頭，身心靈都得到平衡。某日，小梅與五師弟於饅頭店邂逅，發展出一段姻緣。後來她更義助功夫蹴鞠團，於全國大賽的總決賽以四両撥千斤輔助大力金剛腿，踢進了決定性的一球，贏得了冠軍寶座。幾年後，小梅跟五師弟勞燕分飛。她性情大變，竟到京城謀職，參與宮廷事務。雖然民眾對小梅的官僚作風十分反感，但不出幾年她已晉升至內閣大臣，靠的就是四両撥千斤的功夫。後世於是以四両撥千斤形容一個人三言兩語就把責任卸得一乾二淨。

Tai Chi Unloading Force

Archimedes once said, "Give me a lever long enough and a fulcrum to place it, and I shall move the world." From a physics point of view, the so-called theory of using four ounces to move a thousand pounds is based on the principle of leverage. In a similar fashion, the Tai Chi Unloading Force works by drawing, transforming, and unleashing the energy amassed from opponents' movements to cause damage.

Long ago in a small village down by the South, a girl named Mui sold al dente steamed buns that were a favourite among the villagers for their moistness. As she was also a Tai Chi master, she could also knead flour in a way that gave the buns a soft yet firm texture. Falling in love after an encounter with Fifth Brother at her stall one day, she became dedicated to helping his Shaolin soccer team achieve success. She even used her signature move, the Tai Chi Unloading Force, to score a decisive goal in the final match that won the championship title for the team.

Unfortunately, their relationship did not survive and the break-up changed her drastically. Due to her increasingly bureaucratic behaviour, she started down a new career path in politics. Although she was unpopular with the people, Mui only had to put in an equivalent of four ounces of work to become cabinet minister, thanks to the Tai Chi Unloading Force. Generations later, the technique would be quoted in a metaphor to mean relieving one's responsibility by unloading it upon others.

WING CHUN

孔子和耶穌都說過：「念念不忘，必有迴響。有燈，就有人。」如何把傳統、學問與功夫傳承下去？實在是大哉問。詠春這門功夫，又是如何流傳到今時今日這個璀璨的數碼龐克年代呢？

據詠春名師葉問所述：清康熙年間，有廣東人嚴二，因被官府通緝，唯有攜獨女嚴詠春遠走他鄉，以賣豆腐為生。詠春生得花容月貌，少而聰穎，十五歲時，有當地土豪垂涎其姿色，前來逼婚，其父深以為憂。後來結識了少林寺武僧出身之五枚師太，便攜詠春上山，授之以武藝。詠春日夜苦練，學成後返家約土豪比武，將其擊倒。其後五枚師太雲遊四方，臨行前告誡詠春待婚後應發揚武術。詠春婚後乃將武藝傳予夫婿梁氏，其後梁氏再傳予後人。如此這般，終由佛山贊傳予陳華順，陳華順傳予關門弟子葉問，終在香港發揚開來，並通過其子弟如李小龍等人在全球廣泛的傳揚而流傳於世。詠春的出處還有很多版本，在此不贅。至於武術的傳承，相傳葉問某晚夢見自己與五枚師太於大南街茶敘，師太激讚映畫戲的偉大，功夫片在將來會成為熱潮，把傳統武術傳到西方，甚至出現熊貓打功夫的電影，然是有趣。說罷便化作一縷輕煙飄走了。

Wing Chun

Confucius and Jesus once said, "If you think about it from time to time, there will come echoes sublime – where there is light, there is hope…" From traditions to knowledge and martial arts, how are things passed on to the next generation? More specifically, how will Wing Chun continue to survive in the age of the cyberpunk?

According to the Grandmaster Ip Man, the martial art of Wing Chun originated in the Qing dynasty, when a Cantonese man named Yan Er fled to the outskirts of the country after being persecuted by the local government. He brought along his young daughter, Yan Wing Chun, and sold tofu for a living. Charmed by her beauty and intelligence, a local tyrant became infatuated with the fifteen-year-old and forced her to marry him. Desperate, Yan Er became acquainted with a Shaolin female monk named Ng Mui, who led Wing Chun to the mountains and trained her personally. In time, all her hard work paid off as Wing Chun ended up defeating the tyrant in a duel. Later on, having to embark on a pilgrimage, Ng Mui entrusted Wing Chun with the task of passing her skills on. The latter then married into the Liang family, who kept her legacy alive across future generations. As fate would have it, her name-sake technique ended up in the hands of Chen Huashun, who taught the Grandmaster himself. One of the Grandmaster's most well-known disciples, Hollywood star Bruce Lee, then carried on spreading the art of Wing Chun to the rest of the world.

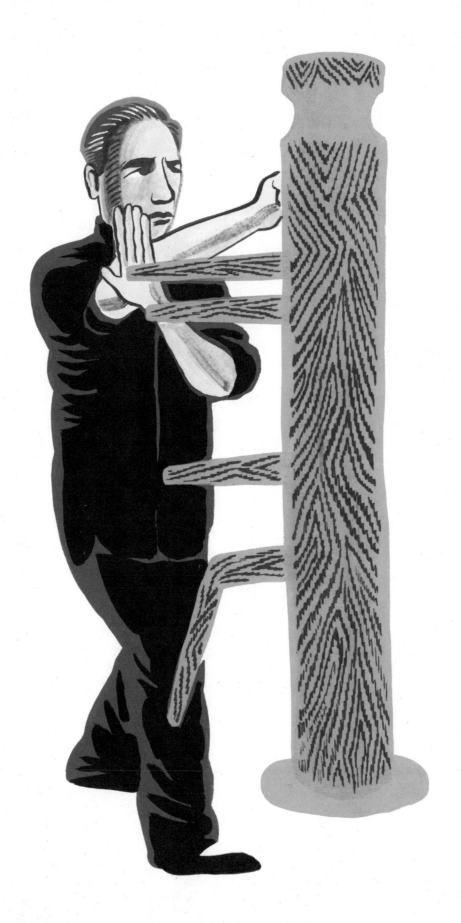

撐

PALM UP HAND

WING HAND

膀

伏

SUBDUING HAND

EIGHT TRIGRAM PALM

八卦掌

中國傳統拳術，以掌法變換和行步走轉為主。因為人們打八卦掌時身法縱橫交錯，隱含四正四隅八個方位，與《周易》八卦圖中的卦象相似，故此掌法被名為八卦掌。傳說是清代武術家董海川在江南「自駕遊」時得到道家修練的啟示，結合武術加以整理而成。

相傳於民國時期，中華武士會會長暨八卦形意門掌門宮寶森宮老爺，偕同徒弟馬三和獨女宮二，從北方來到廣東佛山舉辦引退儀式，並要求跟一位南方高手較量。佛山武術界有人義憤填膺，大聲疾呼：「我哋廣東佬，平時點樣縮骨無品都好，講到打交，幾時認過衰仔？」眾人一致推舉詠春高手葉問出戰。當時著名風月場所金樓的老闆燈叔得悉此事，於是挑了個吉日，請來一批武林高手，特意封葉問試招。當天第一位跟葉問交手的是八卦掌高手、金樓京班班頭三姐。幾招下來，三姐的八卦掌皆被葉問輕易化解，她於是改變策略，轉攻下陰，即廣東俚語「拆祠堂」。只見三姐掌腿並用，向葉問下方的要害一輪猛攻。雖然攻勢悉數被葉問格擋下來，在旁觀戰的一眾武夫卻皆替葉問捏一把汗，內心暗呼：「一定要保住香燈，有燈便有人。」

Eight Trigram Palm

Reflecting its namesake, the Eight Trigram Palm is a traditional Chinese martial art where practitioners perform various palm-led sequences around the Trigram Circle, which is divided into four squares, four corners and eight directions. Dong Haichuan, a Qing-era martial artist, was said to have been inspired by Taoist practices to create this technique during a road trip to Southern China.

At some point during the Republic era, Gong Baosen, the president of the Chinese Warriors Association, made his way to Foshan for a retirement ceremony with his apprentice Ma San and only daughter Gong Er. For some reason or other, he decided to challenge the Southern masters to a duel, enraging the latter. Eventually, Wing Chun master Ip Man was unanimously chosen to fight Gong. When the owner of the famous Golden Pavilion hotel, Uncle Deng, learned of the impending duel, he hired several more top martial artists, thinking, "The more, the merrier." The first person to fight against Ip Man was Sister Three, an Eight Trigram Palm master. When Ip Man deftly blocked her moves, she began to ferociously attack his nether regions in a technique known as "Dismantling the Ancestral Hall", a Cantonese phrase that refers to ending one's bloodline. Luckily, Ip Man skilfully thwarted all her attacks. Although the audience had broken out in a cold sweat, they concurred: "His light must live on – where there is light, there is hope!"

堂祠拆

DISMANTLE ANCESTRAL HALL

SHAPE-WILL FIST

形意拳

動作簡潔樸實、嚴密緊湊、沉着穩健、快速完整。由於形意拳的創始年代及其源流過於久遠，故無確鑿的史料可佐證。有說是達摩老祖所創，有說是岳飛所創，亦有說是明末武將姬際可從槍法演變而來的拳法。

且說葉問為了應戰宮老爺，於金樓與一眾高手試招。緊接着金樓京班班頭三姐與葉問搭手的，是帳房領班先生瑞。關於先生瑞，就連金樓老闆燈叔也不知道他的來歷。有段日子金樓的客人絡繹不絕，收入比以前翻了好幾倍，帳房的工作量大增。然而說也奇怪，帳房的同僚每天還是準時下班。某晚燈叔經過帳房，聽見劈里啪啦之聲響個不停，只見先生瑞正飛快地舞着算盤，十隻手指起如風，落如箭，動作嚴密緊湊、快速鮮明，似乎符合拳理。一問方知這位帳房領班是形意拳高手，一般人要花一天算好的帳，他只需一半時間便能料理妥當。據記載，葉問最終以聽橋破解了先生瑞的半步崩拳。經此一戰，葉問的武藝又提升了不少。正是：「過手如登山，一步一重天。」至於先生瑞，聞說後來遷到香港，把絕技傳給子孫，後代靠形意拳操作西洋電腦，並成立了規模最大的會計師樓。

Shape-Will Fist

Known for its simple, swift, and steady movements, the true origins of the Shape-Will Fist remain unknown. Some say its creator was the Bodhidharma, while others believe that it was Chinese general Yue Fei's brainchild. There are also many who think it was an ancient boxing technique that evolved from the marksmanship of military commander Ji Jike from the Ming dynasty.

After Ip Man defeated Sister Three at the Golden Pavilion hotel duel, a certain Mr. Rui rose to the challenge. A reserved man, Mr. Rui's past was shrouded in mystery, but he had been hired as the head of accounting for the hotel anyway. As business flourished, the accounts department should have been swamped with extra work, but mysteriously, its staff were clocking out punctually every day. One night, the owner of the hotel, Uncle Deng, overheard the sound of rapid and intense clacking coming from the accounts office. Peering inside, he saw Mr. Rui's fingers dancing briskly on the abacus with precision and rhythm. Mr. Rui then revealed that he was a master of the Shape-Will Fist, which explained how he could deal with calculations at jaw-dropping speeds. At the Golden Pavilion, Ip Man used his Tingqiao technique to finish the fight by breaking Mr. Rui's fists – but all was not lost. Legend has it that Mr. Rui ended up moving to Hong Kong and passing the technique on to his descendants, where they eventually combined the Shape-Will Fist with Western computer technology to build the foundations for Hong Kong's largest accounting firm.

半步

崩拳

HUNG FIST

洪拳

關於洪拳的起源有三種說法，一種是洪拳乃清代南方民間秘密結社洪門假託少林所傳習的拳術；另一種是洪拳由元明年間陝西拳術紅拳加上其他拳術演變而來，已有三百多年歷史；還有一種說法是洪拳由清代少林俗家弟子洪熙官始創。

且說葉問先後與八卦掌和形意拳的高手試招，最後則與一位叫鐵橋勇的武夫搭手。關於鐵橋勇，能考證的資料實在不多，只知道他精通洪拳和雜家功夫，外號「一串炮仗」，「雙拳密如雨，快似一掛鞭」。他於金樓擔任何職位、師承何處、婚姻狀況、政治取態等皆不得而知。江湖傳聞，鐵橋勇與外號「鐵橋三」、「廣東十虎」之一的梁坤是親兄弟；亦有人說他們少時一起拜少林僧人為師，是師兄弟，甚至有說鐵橋三其實未死，已練成長生不老之術，混入世俗冷眼看人生，而鐵橋勇其實就是當年的鐵橋三！「詠春三件頭」，洪拳分定寸」，鐵橋勇原本可以與葉問鬥個旗鼓相當，但畢竟拳怕少壯，過了約一柱香時間，鐵橋勇漸感吃力，後來連雜家功夫也使了出來，可惜炮仗依然不響，敗給葉問的詠春三件頭。直至現在，還有人堅信鐵橋勇未死，甚至在某些電影裡仍能看到他的身影。

Hung Fist

There are three theories about the origins of the Hung Fist. The first one posits that it was a boxing technique from the Shaolin Temple that was propagated by a secret society in the South. The second one supposes that it evolved from a 300-year-old boxing technique that originated in Shaanxi. The third one assumes that it was founded by Hong Xiguan, a Shaolin lay disciple from the Qing dynasty.

After beating the masters of the Eight Trigram Palm and Shape-Will Fist, Ip Man faced off with a martial artist known as Master Yong. Not much was known about the latter, other than how proficient he was in the Hung Fist technique. He was even given the nickname Cannonballs, as his fists were as dense as heavy rain and as fast as a light whip. Nobody knew what he was doing at the Golden Pavilion at the time, but it was rumoured that he and Iron Bridge Three, another Hung Fist master, were related by blood. It was also said that they had trained together as Shaolin monks and that Iron Bridge Three was actually an immortal being in disguise. Although Ip Man's Wing Chun and Iron Bridge Three's Hung Fist skills were likely on par with each other, the latter was secretly threatened by Ip Man's vitality. During their duel, Iron Bridge Three ended up losing his momentum, allowing Ip Man to finish him off in a three-step Wing Chun move. Legend has it that he is still alive today, making occasional cameos in random movies.

EIGHT
EXTREMES FIST

八極拳

「八極」意為「發勁可達四面八方極遠之處」。八極拳屬於短打拳法，剛猛暴烈、樸實無華且發力迅猛。在技擊手法上講求硬打硬開，與輕柔內斂的太極拳剛好相互對應。由於八極拳直接狠辣，殺傷力強，因此屢屢成為近代史上保護政要的「大內武術」。成吉思汗、溥儀、特朗普、教宗、英女皇等人的近身侍衛皆習八極拳。

相傳葉問於五十年代來到香港，住在深水埗大南街一帶。當時他結識了一位街坊，其身份神秘，是八極拳高手，街坊都稱他「一線天」，也是剛到香港，在街口經營理髮店。某晚葉問回家路經理髮店，聽見拳風呼呼作響，好奇一看，卻見一線天正在練武。葉問拳癮大發，即時上前切磋，原來一線天曾是地下黨的殺手，因被日軍追捕而逃上火車，幸得一位女貴人相助，替其掩護，才得以順利來到香港。後來一線天決定在香港定居，把理髮店改建成西洋風咖啡廳，很受文藝青年歡迎，每到周末皆客似雲來。許多街坊爭相仿效，武館、布行、皮革店、茶樓，一下子通通變成咖啡廳。然而熱鬧背後，一線天還是每天靜候那位女貴人的出現，希望能親口答謝她的救命之恩。

Eight Extremes Fist

"Eight Extremes" refers to a certain type of energy that can be spread far and wide in all directions, making the Eight Extremes Fist a unique boxing method. Technique-wise, it emphasises brute force and hard hits, making it the preferred martial arts technique of bodyguards for important figures throughout history, such as Genghis Khan, Puyi, Donald Trump, the Pope, and even Queen Elizabeth.

According to legend, Ip Man was living along Tai Nan Street in Sham Shui Po during the 1950s when a mysterious neighbour, dubbed the Razor by locals, set up a barber shop nearby. As Ip Man was walking past the shop one night, the Razor began to pick a fight, demonstrating his mastery in the Eight Extremes Fist. It was then revealed that he was wanted by the Japanese army – having been a hitman for underground triads. He also told the tale of how he eventually escaped his old life with the help of a noble lady. Years after the encounter with Ip Man, the Razor decided to transform his barbershop into a snazzy Western-style café, which eventually became a popular watering hole for young hipsters. Envious of his success, many other businesses began to emulate his business model in Sham Shui Po and beyond. To this day, the Razor is said to be waiting for his noble lady to reappear, hoping to thank her personally for saving his life.

GONG'S STYLE
SIXTY FOUR HANDS

宮家六十四手

相傳可能是演變自八卦掌中的一大絕學「八卦六十四掌」。八卦六十四掌為滄州武人劉德寬所創編，以直趟練習為特色，以技擊、擒拿實用技法為核心。後來經身兼形意與八卦兩大武術的中華武士會會長宮老爺融會貫通，演變成「宮家六十四手」。宮老爺的獨女宮二是此武功的唯一繼承者，她性格剛烈，為報父仇寧願終身不嫁，並且不能再傳武功，宮家六十四手因此絕跡。

宮老爺當年攜同宮二南下，宮二因不服父親敗給葉問，為保宮家聲譽，背着父親與葉問比試。豈料二人不打不相識，竟打出了愛火來。時代列車轟轟地往前開，兩人一直到流落香港才再次相遇，某晚相約於深水埗大南茶室互訴心聲。兩位高手不單功夫了得，文學上的造詣亦非泛泛。「人不辭路，虎不辭山」；「絲不如竹，竹不如肉」；「人生如棋，落子無悔」；「千回百轉，一悲一喜」；「風流本就是個夢」⋯⋯二人一唱一和，文藝腔滿瀉，聽得茶室裡的茶客都醉了。相傳由於二人散發的文藝氣息久久不散，致使大南街一帶發展成為文藝社區，不時有文藝青年去附庸風雅一番。正是：「念念不忘，必有迴響，有一口氣，點一盞燈，有燈就有人。」

Gong's Style Sixty Four Hands

According to legend, Gong's Style is an evolution of the Eight Trigrams Sixty Four Palm – one of the most unique set of sequences to be derived from the Eight Trigrams technique. Created by Cangzhou martial artist Liu Dekuan, it was widely used by members of the Chinese Warriors Association, where its president Gong Baosen eventually developed his own trademarked version called the Sixty Four Hands of the Gong Family or Gong's Style Sixty Four Hands. Gong Er, his only daughter, ended up inheriting the technique and vowed to avenge her father's loss in the Golden Pavilion hotel duel.

Later on, an opportunity arose for Gong Er to defend her family's honour – only to have sparks of a different kind fly during her secret duel with Ip Man. Fate, however, had other plans and they ended up being separated for a time, reuniting after years apart at Sham Shui Po's Tai Nan Tea Room in Hong Kong. As Ip Man and Gong Er were not only Kung Fu masters but also literary intellectuals, the story goes that they exchanged clever proverbs all night long to express their feelings for each other, adding to the already-merry atmosphere of the cosy venue with patrons listening in on their conversation. By combining their skills and interests, they helped to cultivate the artistic vibes of the neighbourhood over time, giving rise to the creative community along Tai Nan Street known as the New Brooklyn today.

THE END 劇終

有燈就有人

太極宗師張三丰曾經講過：「論武功，即使只是曇花一現，但凡有一招半式流傳江湖，皆應被好好保存，莫失莫忘。

俗世中不知邊個高。」

洪陸李白劉關張，麥朱陳江曾郭楊，誰才是個真好漢？古今中外，南北西東，幾多英雄豪傑名留青史；幾多江湖草莽恍如流星，稍縱即逝。名動江湖；有人擅長南拳，有人精於北腿，有人掌風虎虎，有人聲若洪鐘，有人師承名門，有人京劇出身，有人集百家大成，有人自創拳法，有人立志承傳，有人亡命表演，有人擅長翻騰跳躍，有人練肌肉，有人正氣內斂，有人沉迷操湮沒，於是輯錄成紙本印刷品，望後人能銘人溫文儒雅，有人狂放不羈，有人濃眉大眼，記武林長河中曾出現過如此多出眾的高手。有人長髮鼻大，有人黃皮黑髮，有人紅鬚綠眼……所謂「一樣米養百樣人」，正是種種正是：「柔情藏心內，血肉記春秋，大不同類型的武夫，組成了如此多姿多彩，架地留着我的記號。」構龐大的江湖世界。姑勿論武功孰優孰劣，

本書作者顧氏，南方畫家一名，自幼熱愛觀賞功夫影畫戲，曾對銀幕上無數武夫的武藝傾倒，被其身手迷得如痴如醉。某個月夜，顧氏於涼亭把酒問月，酒意漸濃，忽爾雅興大發，隨手執起畫筆於紙上狂舞，竟不自覺記錄了多位武夫的形象。後來畫作輾轉流傳到有心人手中，為了不讓其被時間洪流

Where there is Light,
there is Hope.

Tai Chi master Zhang San-Feng once said, "When it comes to martial arts in this secular world, one will never know what it means to be the best."

What makes a true hero? Across time and far-reaching lands, many a martial artist has left a legacy that will be remembered for generations. Some were experts in Southern Fists, while others were skilled in Northern Kicks. Some could shift energy with their palms, while others shook the earth with a mighty roar. These heroes also came from all walks of life: whether they were disciples of grand masters or trained in Peking Opera. Some practised every technique they could find, while others manifested their very own. Some were determined to pass on their inheritance, while others sadly perished performing dangerous stunts... As people, heroes could be found in all sorts of shapes, sizes and personalities – some were skilled at leaps and jumps, while others were obsessed with getting ripped. Some were righteous and reserved; graceful and cultured, while others were wild, unruly, and partial to life's many pleasures. Some were born with bushy brows and huge eyes, while others grew long tresses to frame pronounced features. Ultimately, regardless of who harnessed its power or how long it has been around for, every martial arts technique should be preserved as an important cultural artefact – not simply forgotten.

A Kung Fu film fanatic ever since he was a child, the author of this book is an artist from the South named Koo. Struck by tipsy inspiration on a moonlit night, he was filled with a sudden determination to replicate the likeness of the legends he grew up admiring. His fervent scribbles on sheets of paper eventually ended up in the hands of someone who saw the potential in the sketches and decided to transform pages into publication, in hopes that future generations would remember that true heroes do indeed exist.

KWAN TAK-HING

1905-1996

關德興

(MBE)

生於廣州，曾深造粵劇，擅演關雲長，後來以演出「黃飛鴻」系列電影而享着譽藝壇。天生健壯有力，相傳能背着七十塊磚頭走一里路。武藝方面，擅長拋繩拉弓等武功，早期曾習洪拳及俠家拳，屬白鶴派兼其他流派。曾受花旗國西部牛仔片影響而練成神鞭絕技，後來更自創無極剛柔拳。正氣俠義的形象深入人心，是武林中人一致推崇的宗師級人馬。

關師傅一生主演超過一百四十部影片，七十七部「黃飛鴻」系列電影。這個系列後來被列入西洋世界之最的「健力士」紀錄，被譽為比西洋特務片「凌凌漆」更長的系列影畫戲。

Kwan Tak-Hing or Master Kwan studied Cantonese Opera and gained popularity after starring in the Wong Fei-Hung films. Built with a strong physique, he was said to be able to walk a mile while carrying 70 bricks. He was also skilled in martial arts involving rope-throwing and bow-pulling. In his early days, he practised the Hung Fist and Xiajia Fist techniques. Inspired by Western cowboy films, he also practised with a whip, eventually creating his own style of Rigid and Soft Boxing. Bearing a righteous and masculine image that was universally admired by martial arts practitioners, Master Kwan starred in more than 140 films. 77 were from the Wong Fei-Hung franchise, which triumphed over the 007 James Bond series in terms of length and earned its place in the Guinness World Records.

SHIH KIEN

1913-2009

石堅

生於廣東，外號「奸人堅」，在「黃飛鴻」電影系列裡經常擔任反派角色，是粵語影畫戲中的老牌反派。其奸笑聲被譽為武林一絕，常被後來者模仿。石堅少年時由於體弱多病，而且一學就學了九年，期間曾習南少林拳及螳螂拳。他特別擅演野獸型角色，當年扮演《倚天屠龍記》中的金毛獅王，霸氣外露；還有在《龍爭虎鬥》中扮演的大反派韓先生，最後以利爪與李小龍展開一場生死鬥，獸性大發，像極了一隻不好惹的野貓。

Shih Kien was nicknamed Villian Kien and often took on the antagonist's role in the Wong Fei-Hung franchise. As a veteran villain in Cantonese films, he was known for his iconic, treacherous laughter that was frequently imitated by latecomers. As a child, Shih practised martial arts to strengthen his frail body, studying the Southern Shaolin Boxing and Praying Mantis Fist techniques for more than nine years. He excelled at playing beast-type roles, such as the golden-haired "lion king" in "The Heaven Sword and Dragon Saber" (1978) and Mr. Han in "Enter the Dragon" (1973), which featured a showdown between Shih and Bruce Lee.

劉家輝

GORDON LIU

1955-Present

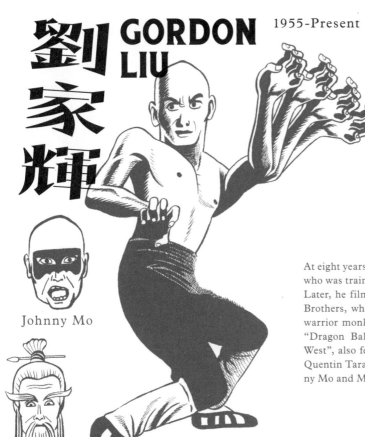

Johnny Mo

Pai Mei

在廣東出生，八歲時拜林世榮的弟子劉湛為師，是黃飛鴻的徒孫，並一直接受劉湛之子劉家良嚴格的正統武術訓練。後來加入邵氏影畫，拍了一系列的功夫戲，其光頭形象亦成功塑造了武僧角色的原型。相傳改篇自《西遊記》的東洋連環圖《龍珠》亦有角色參考其形象設計。千禧年後，外號「鬼才」的西洋影痴塔倫天奴邀請劉師傅出演其仿邵氏懷舊味的復仇影畫《標殺令》，分別扮演殺手強尼莫和武術宗師白眉，令一眾戲迷有機會再次於大銀幕一睹劉師傅的風采。

At eight years old, Gordon Liu became a disciple of Liu Zhan, who was trained by Wong Fei-Hung's disciple Lam Sai-Wing. Later, he filmed a series of Kung Fu dramas with the Shaw Brothers, where his bald head became an iconic trait of the warrior monk. Legend has it that the Japanese comic series "Dragon Ball", which was adapted from "Journey to the West", also featured characters with a similar look. In 2004, Quentin Tarantino even invited Gordon to star as killer Johnny Mo and Master Baimei in his film "Kill Bill".

1934-2013

LAU KAR-LEUNG

劉家良

出身武術世家，父親劉湛是林世榮的弟子。對中國各門派武術均有鑽研。劉師傅是諧趣功夫與茅山殭屍類型影畫戲的正開創者，亦是少數具完整世界觀的作者型功夫片導演。作品走真功夫路線，堅持呈現正宗國術，內容着重中國武術的歷史與傳承，尤其是「武德」的重要，是武林公認真正懂得中國武術，且深具傳統武術精神及華南文化傳統的導演和武術指導。西方俠系影畫戲有句老話：「能力越大，責任越大。」劉師傅的作品格修養，經常強調：「武功越高，越要謙厚。」

Born into a martial arts family, Lau Kar-Leung's father Lau Zhan was a disciple of Lam Sai-Wing. As a pioneer and director of martial arts comedy films and Maoshan vampire genre films who practised several Chinese martial arts himself, he insisted on authenticity with a focus on history and the inheritance of integrity – embodying the popular quote: "With great power comes great responsibility." Lau's works focused on cultivating good character, often emphasising: "The stronger one is, the more humble one should be."

BRUCE LEE

1940-1973

李小龍

Bruce Lee

師徒

Ip Man

考えるな!!感じろ!!

WADAAAAAA!!!

所謂「有諸內者，必形諸外」，李小龍
的造型功架亦自成一格，獨步江湖：
野獸嘶叫、挑撥手勢、輕蔑表情、獵
鷹眼神，拳腳運動有如行雲流水，還有一
雷，把雙截棍舞得恍似疾風迅
身越練越鋼鐵的身形，皆構成了世人
擁戴的所謂「個人風格」。雖然後來模
仿者眾，卻以拙劣模仿者居多，可能才是
學、哲學與美學相互結合，
李小龍一直永垂不朽，名聲能永留史
冊的最大原因。

據典籍記載，當時邵氏一方人強馬
壯，李小龍能夠在高手雲集的武林中
打出一片天，靠的除了是一身橫練真
功夫外，還有一種一般武夫所欠缺的
內涵：於接受西方媒體訪問或撰寫雜
誌文章時總不忘傳達東方思想，發表
了不少富哲學性的理論，啟迪芸芸眾
生突破自我界限。

李小龍在七十年代主演的功夫影畫
《唐山大兄》大獲好評，此後他又主
演了四部功夫影戲，震撼了整個武
林，而且在國際上迅速聲名鵲起。

生於花旗國，成長於香港，譽滿全球。
國際著名華裔武術家及武術指導、截
拳道創始人，也是開創功夫影畫的重
要人物之一。曾拜葉問為師學習詠春
拳，此外還練過洪拳、白鶴拳、蔡李
佛拳、太極拳、譚腿、少林拳等拳種。

A world-famous martial artist and instructor who was born in the States and raised in Hong Kong, Bruce Lee was the founder of Jeet Kune Do and an important figure in Kung Fu movies. As a disciple of Ip Man, Bruce also practised the Hung Fist, Bai He Fist, Cai Lifo Fist, Tai Chi Fist, Tam Tui, Shaolin Fist and other types of boxing. In the 1970s, he starred in the well-received Kung Fu film "The Big Boss" (1971) and quickly rose to international fame after four more films.

The Shaw Brothers Kung Fu films may have been gaining popularity at the time, but Bruce made a name for himself among the masters with his unique perspective. In addition to practising Kung Fu, he always advocated for the traditional Eastern ways of thinking and expressed them through a philosophical lens during media interviews and in magazine articles.

As the saying goes, "every picture tells a story" and Bruce Lee's iconic image speaks for itself – from his unparalleled stature and provocative gestures to his fiery gaze. His lightning speed when swinging his nunchucks and his water-like footwork also became solid elements of his personal style that was embraced by the world. His unique way of combining martial arts, philosophy, and aesthetics may be the biggest reason why Bruce's legendary status has been immortalised in the annals of history.

SIMON YUEN
1912-1979
袁小田
父

生於北平，京劇武生出身，擅長北派武術。來港後成為武打演員及武術指導。是國際級武指袁和平之父。加入戲行初期從事武俠片替身工作，後來參與粵語片製作，成為中國武術指導的師傅，於影畫史上第一位武術指導。常扮演師傅角色，於幾部成龍作品中飾演乞丐造型的師傅角色最深入人心。在東洋連環圖中的很多師傅角色和修練過程都不難發現袁師傅的身影。

The father of world-famous director Yuen Woo-Ping, Simon Yuen began his career in the Peking Opera and excelled at Northern martial arts. After moving to Hong Kong, he became a martial arts actor and instructor, sometimes working as a stunt double before becoming a producer of Cantonese films. He often portrayed the role of a Kung Fu master, with his role as a beggar/master in Jackie Chan's films being the most popular. Due to his fame, he also made frequent cameos as a Kung Fu master in Japanese manga.

Nicknamed the Eighth Master, Simon Yuen's first son was a well-known action film director and stunt director in Hong Kong. He was also the stunt director for notable foreign films such as "The Matrix" and "Kill Bill". While he mainly worked behind the scenes, his light comedy flick "Mismatched Couples" (1985), which he directed and co-starred in with Donnie Yen was a sensational hit that combined Kung Fu with the break-dancing craze of the era.

Simon Yuen's second son trained in the Peking Opera and practised martial arts with his father since childhood. In his early years, he worked as a stuntman until becoming an instructor of martial arts in the late 1960s. Together with his brother Yuen Woo-Ping, they formed the "Yuen Family Class" in the 1980s. He enjoyed making cameos, playing the old homeless beggar who sold the Buddha's Palm manual in Stephen Chow's "Kung Fu Hustle".

袁小田之子，京劇武生。自幼隨父親習武。早年混跡武行，做過替身演員。六十年代末開始負責武術指導，八十年代與胞兄組成「袁家班」。袁祥仁熱衷於客串表演，於周星馳《功夫》一片演，《如來神掌》的老乞丐就是由他扮演。

袁小田之子。外號「八爺」，香港知名電影動作指導和導演。除港片外，亦曾為外語片《廿二世紀殺人網絡》(Matrix) 和《標殺令》(Kill Bill) 擔任動作指導。鮮少於幕前演出，令人較有印象的是他自導自演、與甄子丹合演的《情逢敵手》，一部響應當時霹靂熱潮，糅合了霹靂舞與功夫的輕喜劇。

YUEN CHEUNG-YAN
1957-Present

YUEN WOO-PING
1945-Present

袁祥仁　子　袁和平

羅莽，邵氏電影「張徹系」武打演員，走剛陽路線，以健碩體格縱橫武林。傳聞受李小龍「中國人不是東亞病夫」的電影對白影響決定習武，曾習洪拳、蔡李佛拳及螳螂拳。

除了功夫了得，羅師傅的演技亦不容忽視，如《伊波拉病毒》裡的餐館老闆，既傲慢又狂放。《一代宗師》裡飾演找葉問踢館的武人，幾句對白就演繹出廣東人那種「招積」，實在功力深厚。

千禧年初，羅師傅有份演出的邵氏舊作《少林與武當》中的部份片段被西洋電音組合「化學兄弟」剪輯成音樂錄像《讓自己嗨起來》，新舊交融，效果奇趣。這段奇緣令羅師傅由邵氏廠景的古裝格局一下子跳進了電子舞曲的領域，充滿煥然一新的感覺。當時着實令整個江湖轟動了好一陣子。

Lo Mang is a martial artist known for his strong physique and appearances in the Shaw Brothers films. Inspired by Bruce Lee's notion where "China is not the sick man of the East", he decided to learn Kung Fu, as well as the Hung Fist, Cai Lifo Fist, and Praying Mantis Fist. Aside from martial arts, Lo Mang was also skilled as an actor, having appeared as the restaurant owner in "Outbreak" (1995) and Hei Mian Shen in "The Grandmaster" (2013).

In the 2000s, Lo Mang starred as Tung Chien-Chen in "2 Champions of Shaolin". Some clips from the film were subsequently used in the Chemical Brothers' music video for "Get Yourself High", creating an interesting effect that blended traditional Chinese martial arts with modern electronic dance music.

生於上海，活躍於寶島。走陽剛路線，是張徹導演開創的新武俠浪潮中的第一代明星代表。年少時學過空手道、太極拳。憑武俠電影《獨臂刀》裡驚人的武藝，塑造出俠者形象。相傳王羽戲裡戲外都擅搏擊，有泰山崩於前而色不變的氣勢。

Born in Shanghai, Jimmy Wang kickstarted his career in Formosa and styled himself as a masculine, strong character. He was the first generation of stars in the new wave of martial arts created by director Zhang Che. Having learned Karate and Tai Chi as a child, he showcased his skills in the wuxia film "One-Armed Swordsman" (1967) and solidified his image as a fiery warrior. Rumour has it that Jimmy was as strong as the roles he portrayed in his films – and was always ready for a fight.

LEUNG SIU-LUNG
1948-Present

前　　　後

祖籍廣東、生於香港的武術家，曾習詠春、北派腿法及空手道。拍過多部連續劇及影畫戲，常飾演霍元甲的徒弟陳真。相傳曾於自己武館的梯間遭十多名持利器男子伏擊，最終徒手將對方全部打倒，他自己則只受輕傷。近年最為人所知的演出是於影畫戲《功夫》扮演穿着膠拖鞋爛背心的火雲邪神。

Born in Hong Kong with roots in Guangdong, Leung Siu-Lung studied Wing Chun, the Northern Kick, and Karate. He made numerous appearances in film and television dramas, often assuming the role of Chen Zhen, Huo Yuanjia's apprentice. Legend has it that he was once ambushed by more than a dozen men with sharp weapons in the stairway of his dojo and defeated all of them bare-handed, sustaining only minor injuries. His most well-known performance in recent years was the flip-flopped, vest-wearing Beast in Stephen Chow's "Kung Fu Hustle".

LAM CHING-YING
1952-1997

生於香港，曾拜粉菊花及于占元為師，學習京劇。傳聞李小龍的御用武術指導。乃李小龍拍武戲時不能沒有林正英，否則寧可不開機。林正英在八十年代於《殭屍先生》扮演道長角色，掀起了港台兩地拍攝靈幻殭屍題材的熱潮，從此其形象幾乎與正氣道長劃上等號。他也曾於《敗家仔》扮演沒有眼眉的詠春高手，在影片內展示詠春拳，被許多武林同道推舉為近代武術史上最佳者之一。

Lam Ching-Ying trained under Fen Ju-Hua and Yu Zhan-Yuan in the Peking Opera, and was Bruce Lee's personal martial arts action director. It was even rumoured that Lee would not start filming unless Lam was present. In the 1980s, he played the role of a Taoist priest in "Mr. Vampire" (1995), which set off a wave of Chinese vampire films in Hong Kong and Taiwan. Since then, his image has almost always been equated with the righteous Taoist priest. He also played an eyebrowless Wing Chun master in "The Prodigal Son" (1981). His performance in the film earned him many accolades from the field as one of the best actors in modern martial arts history.

CHAN WAI-MAN
1950-Present

陳惠敏

在香港荃灣長大的客家人，自幼愛習武，學過西洋拳擊。陳惠敏聲音沙啞、個性激烈，常在影畫戲中飾演歹角，如：富翁的打手、一幫之主等。曾代表香港參加東南亞拳賽並贏得冠軍，所以武林有「一拳有陳惠敏，腿有李小龍」的說法。

A Hakka native who grew up in Hong Kong, Chan Wai-Man learned Western boxing and loved training in martial arts as a child. With his hoarse voice and fierce personality, he often portrayed villains in movies and once won the Southeast Asian Boxing Championships representing Hong Kong. There is a saying in martial arts that goes, "Fists of Chan Wai-Man and Kicks of Bruce Lee".

HWANG JANG-LEE
1950-Present

黃正利

在東瀛出生的韓國人，曾習太極拳、跆拳道，並取得黑帶九段認證，成為「祖師黃正利」。七十年代著名功夫演員，歹角中的皇者，以三白眼及兩撇鬍子的造型而為人認識。相傳是東洋連環圖《龍珠》裡的殺手角色桃白白之原型。

A Korean born in Dongying, Hwang Jang-Lee practised the Tai Chi Fist and Taekwondo, becoming the "Patriarch Hwang Jang-Lee" after obtaining the 9th dan black belt certification. In the 1970s, he became known for his protrayals of evil characters in Kung Fu films, solidified by his sinister gaze and iconic moustache. He was even said to be the inspiration for Mercenary Tao, a killer in the Japanese manga "Dragon Ball".

WANG LUNG-WEI
1949-Present

王龍威

山東狂人，走北方硬漢路線。相傳曾習洪拳、泰拳、西洋拳，亦是剛柔會空手道黑帶。加入戲行後常隨劉家良研習洪拳，曾參與大量張徹及劉家良導演的影畫戲，常演歹角，幾十年下來演盡了壞人。較少有的正派角色是於劉家良導演的《武館》中扮演一位着重武德、一心以武會友的北方高手，在最後一場戲與劉家輝於窄巷的比武，堪稱經典。

王龍威在八十年代自編自導「都市劈友劇」《尖東梟雄》，全片大灑狗血，血腥程度堪比東洋導演深作欣二。

Nicknamed the Shandong Madman, Wang Lung-Wei is known for his tough and chiselled appearance. It is said that he used to practise the Hung Fist, Muay Thai, and Western boxing; and even had a black belt in Karate. After getting into theatre acting, he trained in the Hung Fist with Lau Kar-Leung and participated in a large number of film and television dramas directed by Zhang Che and Lau himself, often acting as villains. In a rare portrayal of the good guy, Wang also played a devoted Northern master in Lau's "Martial Club" (1981), where he fought Gordon Lau in a scene that is considered a classic in film history today. In the 1980s, he wrote and directed the cult film "Hong Kong Godfathers", which was known for its gruesome and gory scenes that rivalled that of Japanese director Fukasaku Kinji.

YUEN WAH
1950-Present

生於香港，師承京劇表演藝術家于占元，與元秋及洪金寶等同為「七小福」成員。曾習詠春和太極拳。早期主要擔任替身演員，被李小龍欽點為翻跟斗的指定替身。八十年代開始活躍於大銀幕，在洪金寶作品《東方禿鷹》中扮演大反派，角色幾乎沒有對白，瘦削陰森、表情詭異、動作狠辣。後來於多部作品皆飾演反派。於《功夫》一片扮演小男人包租公楊過。最離奇的一次演出，是於《殭屍先生》一片中飾演需要大量跳躍動作的殭屍。

Yuen Wah trained under Peking Opera artist Yu Zhan-Yuan and was part of "The Painted Faces" group with Yuen Qiu and Sammo Hung. He studied Wing Chun and Tai Chi, mainly acting as a stand-in actor in his younger days. He was then appointed by Bruce Lee as the latter's designated stand-in for somersaults. In the 1980s, he became active on the big screen and played the villain in Sammo Hung's "Eastern Condors" (1987), as well as in many other works. In "Kung Fu Hustle" (2004), he played Yang Guo, or the Landlord of the Walled City. One of his most bizarre performances was in "Mr. Vampire" (1985), where he demonstrated his jumping skills as a hopping creature of the night.

YUEN QIU
1950-Present

生於香港，曾跟隨于占元學習京劇，屬「七小福」成員之一。年輕時主要擔任女替身，曾有份演出西洋特務影畫《凌凌漆大戰金槍客》。後來於八十年代嫁作人婦，隱退江湖。十八年後，因陪師妹到電影《功夫》試鏡而受到導演周星馳的注意，獲周氏力邀演出城寨包租婆一角，與元華組成夫妻檔。相傳元秋為求神似胖婦形象，在兩個月內增加了近十四公斤。後來包租婆一角獲得極大迴響，元秋於是重出江湖，再次活躍於幕前。

Yuen Qiu studied Peking Opera with Yu Zhan-Yuan and is a member of "The Painted Faces" group. In her early years, she often played the female stand-in, performing in the spy film "The Man with the Golden Gun" (1974). She got married and retired in the 1980s, only to return 18 years later when she was noticed by director Stephen Chow while accompanying her sister to the auditions for "Kung Fu Hustle" (2004). Apparently, Yuen Qiu gained nearly 14 kilos in two months for her role as the stout Landlady, which eventually became an iconic character in the film. Having received critical acclaim for her portrayal, Yuen Qiu eventually returned to the Kung Fu scene.

生於香港，外號「三毛」，武林中人尊稱「大哥大」。參與過大量電影工作，因身形肥胖但身手靈活而於武林中佔一席位。九歲時以童星身份加入戲行，後跟于占元學習京劇武術，是「七小福」中的大師兄。除練習京劇武術之外，也練過跆拳道和詠春。洪金寶屬於全方位型的戲行工作者，擔任過演員、導演、動作設計以至出品人，參與的影畫以諸功夫片為主，作品風格主打節奏輕快、人物可愛、邪不勝正。他設計的動作場面常有奇思妙想，如「福星」系列及《葉問二》的圓桌戰等。

洪金寶非常願意提拔有實力的新人，如在八五年監製的《皇家師姐》中，便大膽起用當時還是新人的楊紫瓊和洋人女武生羅芙洛為主角，亦因此成功開創了女武生影畫戲風潮。

Nicknamed Sammo and honoured as the "Big Brother" of martial arts, Sammo Hung worked in numerous films despite his large frame and prided himself in his agility. At the age of nine, he got into acting and trained in Peking Opera and martial arts under Yu Zhan-Yuan. Although he practised Taekwondo and Wing Chun, Sammo is an all-round actor who has also served as a director, action designer, and producer. The films he participated in were mainly Kung Fu comedies with whimsical scenes and lovable characters. He became known for his clever use of environments and props, as seen in the classic round table battle in "Ip Man II" (2010). Sammo was also eager to promote newcomers with potential, having cast newcomer Michelle Yeoh and foreign martial artist Cynthia Rothrock as protagonists in his film "Yes Madam" (1985) – creating a new wave of women-led martial arts films.

SAMMO HUNG
1952-Present

洪金寶

本名房仕龍。生於香港，是著名武生、武術指導、導演和監製。特徵長髮大鼻，擅演功夫小子角色，但並未學過正統武術，演出風格以肉緊表情和玩命動作見稱。因為生性頑皮，念完小學一年級便輟學。後跟隨于占元學習京劇，是「七小福」成員之一。七十年代因李小龍風潮而改藝名為成龍，嘗試模仿李小龍演出風格，但事業發展未見突破。

七八年主演的《蛇形刁手》和《醉拳》，改走諧趣功夫路線，結果反應極佳。後來有份自導自演的《龍少爺》當中一場踢毽子比賽異常精彩，算是早期糅合運動比賽與功夫的影畫戲。成龍作品一向以跳躍翻騰和高難度動作為賣點，曾於訪問中大方承認動作設計參考了西方演員巴斯特基頓和差利卓別靈。

Born Fang Shi-Long, Jackie Chan is a famous martial artist, martial arts instructor, director, and producer characterised by his iconic hair and big nose. While he never trained in orthodox martial arts, he was known for his exaggerated facial expressions and dangerous stunts. As a disobedient kid, he dropped out of primary school and pursued a career in acting and Peking Opera under Yu Zhan-Yuan, becoming a member of "The Painted Faces" group. In the 1970s, he changed his stage name to Jackie Chan and tried to imitate Bruce Lee's performance style to break through but to no avail. In 1978, he starred in "Snake in the Eagle's Shadow" (1978) and "Drunken Master" (1978), switching his strategy to portray martial arts comedy characters and inevitably finding success. Later, he directed and starred in "Dragon Lord" (1982), which fused the sport of shuttlecock kicking with Kung Fu. Jackie's works have always been based on jumping, tumbling, and complicated stunts. He once admitted in an interview that his sequences were inspired by the works of Buster Keaton and Charlie Chaplin.

成龍

JACKIE CHAN

1954-Present

元彪
YUEN BIAO
1957-Present

A famous martial artist who learned Wing Chun, Yuen Biao studied Peking Opera from the age of five under Yu Zhan-Yuan and was a member of "The Painted Faces" group. With his fit and slender frame, he was good at playing boyish roles in the early days. In 1979, he became famous for his starring role in "Knockabout", which kicked off his career. A frequent co-star of Sammo Hung and Jackie Chan, he starred in "The Champions" (1983), a successful novel film that integrated martial arts with football. After its success and that of "Peacock King" (1988), he became a lovable icon among the Japanese due to his overbite and even released three music albums in the country.

生於香港，著名武生，曾學過詠春拳。五歲時便已向于占元拜師學習京劇，是「七小福」成員之一。身形瘦削，身手比洪金寶和成龍多一分矯健，早期擅演小子型角色。七九年憑主演《雜家小子》成名，之後多部作品均與洪金寶和成龍合演，可說是後李小龍時代港產片最強勁的動作影星。八三年主演的影畫戲《波牛》，首次將武術融入足球運動，娛樂性十足。戲中踢球的場面，可媲美同時期成龍自導自演的《龍少爺》那段經典的踢毽子比賽。由於長有一顆齙牙，有幾分東洋人的感覺，加上影畫《波牛》和《孔雀王子》的成功，令元彪在東洋國的人氣非常高，甚至在當地推出過三張唱片，是當年京劇訓練的有趣輸出。

KARA WAI
1960-Present

惠英紅

生於香港，滿洲正黃旗後裔。眼神凌厲、顴骨高凸、神情外露、英姿勃勃，端的是一副女中豪傑模樣。以剛強俠女形象縱橫武林數十載，因為有舞蹈底子，故身手矯健，而且有一種武林欠缺的靈動柔美。十九歲獲劉家良師傅提拔，演出多部功夫影畫戲，是劉家班的堅實成員之一。廿二歲那年憑《長輩》一片榮獲第一屆香江影畫戲金人獎最佳花旦之銜頭。相傳惠英紅曾因不能接受韶華漸去而絕跡江湖多年，可幸後來獲不少武林同道支持而克服心魔，重出江湖。

A descendant of the Manchurian Plain Yellow Banner Clan, Kara Wai was born with a natural, warrior-like appearance. With a hawkish gaze, sharp cheekbones, and a heroic stance, she shaped her image as a fierce fighter through her decades of martial arts training. As a trained dancer, she also honed a particular kind of agility and flexibility that martial artists usually lack. At 19, she was promoted by Lau Kar-Leung to perform in a number of Kung Fu films. At 22, she won Best Actress in the first Hong Kong Film Awards with "My Young Auntie" (1975). Rumour has it that Kara once disappeared from the film scene for many years as she could not accept her ageing appearance. Fortunately, she returned on screen again with support from her fellow martial artist friends.

LEE HOI-SANG
1941-Present

李海生

詠春拳高手，師承葉問入室弟子招允，亦有接觸柔道和西洋健身。邵氏龍虎武師出身，外號「打手王」，以一身發達肌肉打出名堂。相傳曾有一天吃下十多個雞蛋以增強肌肉的驚人舉動。曾跟多位武生交過手，如劉家輝、洪金寶、成龍、黃正利。早期以扮演反派為主，而且大多為武功高強的最終頭目。也有少數正派角色，如在《少林三十六房》中扮演的戒律院住持，以一雙柳葉刀與劉家輝的三節棍鬥得難分難解，為武林同道激讚的精彩比武之一。

A Wing Chun master who trained under Ip Man's disciple Zhao Yun, Lee Hoi-Sang is also experienced in Judo and Western fitness training. Nicknamed the King of Fighters, he is famous for his well-developed muscles which have been attributed to the rumour that he ate more than a dozen eggs in a day to gain muscle. He has also duelled against many martial artists such as Gordon Liu, Sammo Hung, Jackie Chan and Huang Zhengli. In the early days, he mainly played villainous roles with the exception of a few heroes.

CHIN SIU-HO
1963-Present

錢小豪

CHIN KA-LOK
1965-Present

錢嘉樂

兄　弟

香港出生，十歲起跟隨大聖劈掛門的冼師傅學拳，曾多次參加擂台比武。七十年代末被邵氏名導演張徹納入旗下，演出大量功夫片。之後因於影畫戲《殭屍先生》扮演道士徒弟一角而受矚目，另外於《不夜天》與袋鼠搏擊亦一度成為武林話題。

香港出生的武生、武術指導及主持人，錢小豪的胞弟。輟學後經兄長引薦成為龍虎武師，進入戲行學做武術指導。後來獲洪金寶賞識，成為洪家班當年最年輕的龍虎武師，一度是「四大天王」劉德華的御用替身。拍攝過幾部領銜主演的影畫戲，後來因幕前演出沒有太大起色而轉投公仔箱，參與遊戲節目《焦急無敵獎門人》，並被敕封為「獎老」。

At the age of ten, Chin Siu-Ho learned boxing from Master Xian and has participated in multiple fighting matches since then. In the late 1970s, he was cast by Shaw Brothers director Zhang Che in numerous Kung Fu films. Later on, he caught his break by playing the role of a Taoist apprentice in "Mr. Vampire" (1985). His fight with a kangaroo in "Killer's Nocturne" (1987) also became an instant hit in the world of martial arts.

Hong Kong-born martial artist, instructor, and host Chin Ka-Lok is Chin Siu-Ho's younger brother. Having dropped out of school, the elder Chin had recommended that he become a martial artist. Eventually, he was noticed by Sammo Hung and became the youngest martial artist in the latter's team. Since then, he has had the leading role in several film and television dramas. After a career rut, he decided to switch to the entertainment scene, making a comeback in the game show "The Super Trio".

MOON LEE
1965-Present

李賽鳳

香港出生的女武生，為八九十年代香港動作片的代表女星之一。相貌甜美可人，被武林中人譽為動作片中的天使，代表作亦名為《天使行動》。於徐克作品《新蜀山劍俠》中扮演一位青春可人的少女劍客，此後演出了多部動作影畫。九十年代後期淡出江湖，開設舞蹈學堂培育人才。

自小學習中國舞蹈，亦曾習北派功夫，此手腳柔軟靈活。

A martial artist born in Hong Kong, Moon Lee was one of the most iconic Hong Kong action stars in the 1980s and 1990s. With her sweet appearance, she was also affectionately nicknamed the Angel of Action Movies. Having learned Chinese dance and Northern Kung Fu as a child, she is inherently flexible and agile. In Tsui Hark's "Zu: Warriors from the Magic Mountain" (1983), she played a young swordswoman in a role that led to many other appearances. She retired from showbiz in the late 1990s and opened a dance school.

CHIU CHI-LING
1943-Present

趙志凌

香港出生的著名武生，武林中人尊稱他為「趙師傅」。洪拳黃飛鴻的第三代傳人，是第一代傳人林世榮的徒孫，亦是當今世界首屈一指的洪拳大師。他創立的國際洪拳趙志凌國術健身會，全世界弟子超過二十萬人，在武林擁有極大影響力。趙師傅曾參與過不少幕前演出，最為矚目的是於周星馳作品《功夫》中扮演一位隱退江湖、帶點娘娘腔的鐵線拳高手裁縫師傅。除了功夫了得，趙師傅戰戰兢兢的表情亦深受觀眾喜愛。

Known as Master Chiu, Chiu Chi-Ling is a third-generation descendant of Hung Fist master Wong Fei-Hung, eventually becoming a master himself. He also founded the Chiu Chi-Ling International Hung Gar Kung Fu Association, which has more than 200,000 disciples around the globe. Master Zhao has participated in many on-screen performances, most notably in Stephen Chow's "Kung Fu Hustle" (2004) as the Tekken master Tailor Sheng. In addition to his Kung Fu skills, his trembling expressions have also been loved by audiences.

馮克安

FUNG HAK-ON
1950-2016

生於廣東，香港武生，曾習白鶴拳和八卦掌。出身於演藝世家，父親馮峰是三四十年代著名的粵劇小生。馮克安自小就跟隨父親進入戲行，六七十年代開始進入劉家班做龍虎武師，七十年代末轉投成家班，常與洪金寶和成龍合作。由於面目陰森，故常演歹角。九十年代後期開始淡出幕前，偶爾會客串。零四年便於周星馳作品《功夫》中客串能夠琴發魔音的古琴二人組其中一角，並與趙師傅在裁縫店有一場比武戲，招招狠辣，功架俱在。

Born in Guangdong and raised in Hong Kong, Fung Hak-On is the son of famous Chinese Opera star Fung Fung and was introduced to the screen at an early age. He practiced the Bai He Fist and Eight Trigram Palm, and joined Lau's class as a martial artist in the 1960s and 1970s, often working with Sammo Hung and Jackie Chan. Because of his sinister expressions, he frequently played evil antagonists. In the late 1990s, he faded from the scene and only made occasional cameos. In "Kung Fu Hustle" (2004), he was one of the Ancient Piano Duo that duelled against Master Chiu in the tailor's shop.

DICK WEI

1952-Present

生於寶島，著名武生，自幼愛武。身材魁梧、高大，以飾演狠、霸、猛的反派角色獨步武林。曾經在寶島入伍，獲得陸軍上校軍銜，而且特別擅長跆拳道，是寶島海陸兩軍的空手道、跆拳道和國術的總教頭，實戰能力甚強。也擅長刀術、劍術和棍術。八十年代常於洪金寶和成龍的影畫戲裡扮演頭目、保鏢、金牌打手，或軍人一類的反派角色。他最為武林稱頌的角色，要數成龍作品《A計劃》中的海盜頭領羅三炮：目光如炬、霸氣外露，加上渾身肌肉和刺青，一出場已有一種懾人氣勢。結局時與洪金寶、成龍和元彪同場較量，以一敵三，端的是一場精彩絕倫的比拼。

Born in Formosa, Dick Wei trained in martial arts since childhood. With a burly and tall appearance, he often plays the role of ruthless, tyrannical, and fierce antagonists. He once joined the army and reached the rank of colonel, specialising in hand-to-hand combat. Besides being a chief instructor of Karate, Taekwondo, and martial arts, he is also skilled with a knife, sword, and pole. In the 1980s, he often played villainous roles like bodyguards or soldiers in the films of Sammo Hung and Jackie Chan. Covered in tattoos and rippling muscles, one of his most well-known roles was the pirate king in Jackie Chan's "Project A" (1983).

狄威

MICHELLE YEOH

1962-Present

An internationally-renowned martial artist of Malaysian-Chinese descent, Michelle Yeoh has received multiple international honours including the Malaysian Dato' and Commander of the National Order of the Legion of Honour of France. Well-rounded in talent, she trained in ballet, painting, and piano from the age of four, and is also skilled in swimming and badminton. In the 1980s, she went to pursue her career in Hong Kong, where she became known for her short hair, bronze skin, and defined features. She starred alongside Cynthia Rothrock in her first action film "Yes, Madam" (1985) produced by Sammo Hung, kickstarting a new wave of women-led martial arts films. According to legend, she trained with Dick Wei for half a year, punching sandbags and practising her kicks every day. After starring in Ang Lee's "Crouching Tiger, Hidden Dragon" (2000), she began venturing into arthouse films. In 2022, she starred in her most representative and successful work, "Everything Everywhere All at Once", a science fiction film that combines Kung Fu and surrealism in a multiverse setting.

馬來西亞華裔，國際知名女武生。擁有拿督、法蘭西騎士榮譽勳章等多項名銜。自小已文武兼備，從四歲開始學習西洋芭蕾舞、繪畫和鋼琴，也擅長游泳和羽球。八十年代到香港發展，早期以短髮示人，一身古銅色肌膚和骨感臉型，於當時而言是極富時代氣息的女武生。第一部主演的動作戲是與洋人女武生羅芙洛合演、由洪金寶監製的《皇家師姐》，因反應不俗，成功開創了女武生影畫戲風潮。相傳她為了武打戲曾跟狄威習武半年，每天練習打沙包和踢腿。千禧年出演李安導演的《臥虎藏龍》，其時亦開始轉型接拍文藝片。二二年參與被譽為「形而上學腦洞大開」的影畫《媽的多重宇宙》，一人分飾多個次元的自己，是一部糅合功夫與神怪的科幻片，被她視為個人代表作。

楊紫瓊

JOYCE GODENZI
1965-Present

高麗虹

Miss Hong Kong 1984

香港出生，中澳混血兒。大學畢業後成為時裝模特兒。八四年參加香江小姐選美大賽並當選冠軍。後來決心成為一位女武生。高麗虹在八七年於洪金寶作品《東方禿鷹》中扮演一位英勇善戰的東埔寨游擊隊隊員，一眾武林高手對她刮目相看。相傳與洪金寶的合作不僅令她對中國功夫產生了興趣，更對洪金寶本人更共諧連理。

Born in Hong Kong, Joyce Godenzi is of mixed Chinese-Australian heritage and became a fashion model after graduating from university. In 1984, she won the Miss Hong Kong beauty pageant and decided to pursue martial arts under Sammo Hung. In 1987, she played a heroic Cambodian guerrilla girl in Sammo Hung's "Eastern Condors" – her outstanding performance changing the public's perception of her abilities. Her collaboration with Sammo Hung not only ignited her love for Chinese Kung Fu, but also for Sammo himself – and the two eventually married.

CYNTHIA ROTHROCK
1957-Present

羅芙洛

花旗國女武生，碧眼金髮，外號「最打得美魔女」。動作風格快狠準、實淨而不花俏。十三歲開始習武，精通刀、槍、劍、棍、空手道、唐手道、跆拳道、鷹爪功、北少林拳及五形拳等，於中國和韓國的六個武術流派中取得了黑帶的地位，是武林中少見精通多項武藝的洋人。八十年代到香港發展，拍攝了多部洪家班的動作戲。八十年代到香港發展，拍攝了多部洪家班的動作戲。後來香港的動作戲日落西山，羅芙洛於是回花旗國戲行繼續發展，並設館授徒。

With her blonde hair and blue eyes, American warrior Cynthia Rothrock was nicknamed the Feisty Enchantress. Having started training in martial arts at the age of 13, she was known for her excellent agility and precise strikes. She is also skilled in knives, spears, swords, poles, Karate, Tang Shoudo, Taekwondo, Eagle Claw, the Northern Shaolin Fist, and Wuxing Fist. Cynthia also obtained a black belt in six martial arts schools across China and South Korea. In the 1980s, she pursued acting in Hong Kong, starring in many action flicks and dramas. When Hong Kong action films went out of style, she returned to the States to set up her own school and continued her acting career there.

DONNIE YEN

1963-Present

廣東出生，香港成長，國際級武生，外號「丹爺」。後來因票房成績超越西方俠客鋼鐵人，被外界冠以「宇宙最強」之外號。武功凌厲迅猛、爆發力強、充滿力度，於動作之中巧妙融入西方的綜合格鬥技元素。角色演繹多以冷面示人，早期曾飾演不少反派終極頭目角色，後期則只演英雄人物。

由於母親是一位太極高手，丹爺自幼已跟隨她學習北少林拳及太極拳。相傳丹爺有一項神奇技能，能完美重現曾看過的功夫片段中的所有動作，同時逐步學習多種風格的武術。後來因緣際會，得到國際級武指袁和平賞識，開始進入戲行參與幕前演出。雖然演過不少精彩的武打場面，但發展一直不慍不火。直到後來與洪金寶合演《殺破狼》一片，動作設計加入大量西方綜合格鬥技元素，不但令丹爺再次受到矚目，亦再次帶起武術電影畫熱潮。零八年，於《葉問》一片飾演詠春大師葉問。影畫上映後轟動武林，四十五歲的丹爺終於迎來武術生涯的高峰。後來他不單雄霸了整個武林，甚至衝出亞洲，衝出宇宙，成為第一個演出「星球大戰」系列的亞裔演員，是武林中為人津津樂道的勵志故事。

Born in Guangdong and raised in Hong Kong, Donnie Yen is an international martial artist that was dubbed the universe's strongest when his box office sales surpassed that of Iron Man. He is known for his signature combat skills, which incorporate Western mixed martial arts with Kung Fu, resulting in fierce, explosive, and strong movements. In the early days, he played many evil mob bosses and villains, but switched to righteous hero-type roles later on.

Donnie's mother was a Tai Chi master, which likely attributed to his training in Northern Shaolin Boxing and Tai Chi since childhood. Legend has it that he can perfectly replicate all the movements in Kung Fu clips he has seen. His skills even drew the appreciation of international martial arts master Yuen Woo-Ping, which led to his on-screen debut. Although he performed in many riveting martial arts films, Donnie found it hard to catch a break. It was only through "Kill Zone" (2005), where he incorporated Western mixed martial arts elements into action design, that he found the limelight and sparked a new wave of martial arts films. In 2008, he caused a sensation in the film industry with his excellent performance as the Grandmaster in "Ip Man", which ushered in the peak of his martial arts career. Later, he not only dominated the Asian martial arts scene but even became the first Asian actor to perform in the Star Wars film franchise.

BILLY CHOW

1958-Present

周比利

加拿大出生，世界拳王。外號「北腿王」，擅長腿法，腿勁凌厲且具爆發力。相傳其拳擊生涯從未被技術性擊倒過。五歲開始學習空手道，八五年獲自由搏擊世界冠軍。同年加入戲行，主要參與洪家班的影畫戲。由於相貌兇狠威猛，幾乎所有角色都是反派金牌打手或最後頭目。於《精武英雄》中扮演一位軍官，與李連杰的對打戲長而密，每記殺着皆癲狂無情，恍如一部不能停止的殺人機器。

A Canadian-born world champion nick-named the King of Northern Kicks, Billy Chow excels at footwork and is known for his strong and explosive kicks. Legend has it that he has never been defeated in his boxing career in terms of technicality. He started to learn Karate at the age of five and won the world championship of free kickboxing in 1985. In the same year, he made his on-screen debut under Sammo Hung. Due to his fierce appearance, almost all the characters he plays are villains or final bosses. He played a military commander in "Fist of Legend" (1994), where his tense duel with Jet Li was described as mad and ruthless – likening him to an unstoppable killing machine.

KENNETH LO

1959-Present

盧惠光

與勁力一次登峰造極的展現。打，腿法收放自如，步步進逼，能踢出極多高難度腿法，是柔軟度、耐力拳二》內扮演的反派，尾段與成龍對法。光叔真正受武林矚目始於《醉演出，更負責保鑣工作，任其左右護際會進入戲行，因格鬥技巧高超而獲選手的肋骨打到插進肺裡。後來因七連冠，最勇猛的一次曾把一個澳門於八十年代曾經在香港泰拳比賽取得學習跆拳道，後來更順道學習泰拳。號「光叔」。相傳因自小崇拜李小龍而生於寮國，泰國華僑，香港武生，外

成龍賞識加入成家班，不但參與幕前

Laos-born Kenneth Lo is of Thai-Chinese descent and underwent martial arts training in Hong Kong, Nicknamed Uncle Guang, it was said that he learned Taekwondo and Muay Thai because he admired Bruce Lee as a child. In the 1980s, he won seven consecutive championships in Hong Kong Muay Thai competitions – punching an opponent so hard that he caused the latter's broken rib to stab his own lung. Later on, Kenneth entered showbusiness and was noticed by Jackie Chan for his superb fighting skills. Not only was he an actor, but a bodyguard as well. He garnered a lot of attention for his portrayal as the villain in "Drunken Master II" (1994), where he fought against Jackie using extremely complicated kick-sequences. Aside from his strength, the scene also showcased his endurance and dexterity.

KURATA YASUAKI

1946-Present

倉田保昭

生於東京，東洋武生。六歲開始跟父親學習空手道，具備空手道七段、柔道三段、合氣道二段等資格。生就一副沉着、銳利、威猛的面孔，憑真功夫於武林闖出名堂。七八十年代開始活躍於香港影壇，以扮演反派為主，而大部份都是「東洋高手」一類的設定。據典籍記載，倉田於《夏日福星》中曾與洪金寶和成龍對戰，把一對鐵尺耍得快而密。後來於《精武英雄》與李連杰的比武更被奉為教科書級別的打鬥場面。

Tokyo-born Kurata Yasuaki began learning Karate with his father at the age of six and achieved the 7th dan in Karate, 3rd dan in Judo, and 2nd dan in Aikido. Born with defined features and a fierce demeanour, he made a name for himself in martial arts with his Kung Fu skills. In the 1970s and 1980s, he ventured into the Hong Kong film industry, mainly playing villainous roles. Kurata once fought against Sammo Hung and Jackie Chan using a pair of iron rulers in "Twinkle Twinkle Lucky Stars" (1985). His fight with Jet Li in "Fist of Legend" is regarded as a textbook example of a classic fight scene.

MICHIKO NISHIWAKI

1957-Present

西脇美智子

A Japanese martial artist nicknamed the Yamaguchi Momoe of Fitness, Michiko Nishiwaki trained in gymnastics since childhood and became a well-known figure in the Japanese fitness industry. She has also won three consecutive championships in bodybuilding and weightlifting. In the 1980s, she ventured into the Hong Kong film industry, often typecast as villains due to her straight-faced appearance. For her debut, she played a female thug in "My Lucky Stars" (1985), where she shocked audiences by revealing rippling muscles under her kimono. One of her most famous performances was at the beginning of "God of Gamblers" (1989), where she stunned viewers even without putting up a fight.

東洋出生的女武生，外號「健身界山口百惠」。自小接受體操訓練，入戲行前已是東洋健身界的知名人物，曾連續三次獲得健美及舉重冠軍。八十年代開始進入香港戲行發展，由於外表冷峻無情，角色多以受差使的反派為主。初出道時於《福星高照》扮演一位女打手，褪下和服後展現一身肌肉，讓台下觀眾驚訝萬分。而最著名的演出則是於《賭神》開首與賭神賭骰子那場戲，短短幾分鐘，沒有武打場面，卻氣勢懾人。

JET LI

1963-Present

李連杰

生於北京，中國武術家，外號「功夫皇帝」。相傳其懂得的武術套路非常多，被國際級武指袁和平譽為「功夫字典」。早期以扮演正派俠義角色為主，九十年代初以「黃飛鴻」系列奠定其一線武生地位。由張三豐、洪熙官、霍元甲，到黃飛鴻，在他事業高峰時期，幾乎一人演盡所有宗師級人物。打入西方夢工場後，則嘗試反派角色，是少數亦正亦邪的一線武生。動作風格富傳統美，敏捷漂亮、華美如舞，具備一種罕見的古典儒雅，是武林中數一數二的高手。

李連杰八歲開始進入體育學堂成為武術精英，曾連續獲得五次中國全國武術大會冠軍。十九歲於其處女作《少林寺》扮演武僧覺遠，武藝表現一鳴驚人。九十年代，被導演徐克相中，重新演繹武林傳奇人物黃飛鴻，不單比關德興的版本更年輕，拳腳動作亦更緊湊，加上音樂才子黃露重新改篇的《將軍令》、徐克對美術設計的一絲不苟，令新版《黃飛鴻》公映後震驚武林，武林中人對李連杰的演繹亦讚譽有加。《黃飛鴻》某程度上再次掀起功夫武俠熱潮，單是李連杰便於短短五年時間主演了十七部武俠影畫戲。後來熱潮退卻，他轉往西方夢工場大展拳腳，其東方武夫形象亦很受西方愛戴。

Born in Beijing, Jet Li was nicknamed Kung Fu Emperor and Kung Fu Dictionary by Yuen Wo-Ping due to his expansive knowledge of martial arts routines. In the early days, he mainly played the role of the honest and chivalrous protagonist. His most representative role was Wong Fei-Hung, the eponymous hero of the film. Having established his world-class martial arts status with the franchise in the early 1990s, he then played other highly sought-after protagonist roles such as Zhang Sanfeng, Hong Xiguan and Huo Yuanjia at the peak of his career. After venturing into Hollywood, he tried his hand at playing the role of the villain, which was regarded as a rare move for him. Nonetheless, his movements were fluid, elegant, and swift – earning him the reputation as one of the best masters in martial arts history.

Jet Li began training in martial arts at the age of eight, having won five consecutive championships in the China National Wushu Conference. At the age of 19, he played the fighting monk Jueyuan in his debut film "The Shaolin Temple" (1982) and became an instant star with his superior fighting skills. In the 1990s, he was chosen by director Tsui Hark to reinterpret the legendary Wong Fei-Hung. Not only was he younger than Kwan Tak-Hing's version of the role, but his moves were also more solid and well-grounded. In addition to the rewritten score by musical genius Huang Fei, Tsui Hark's meticulous art direction also gave the franchise a facelift. Having earned praise from the martial arts circle for his interpretation of Wong Fei-Hung, Jet Li went on to star in 17 films in just five years. When the craze subsided, he moved on to Hollywood to develop his career.

HUNG YAN YAN
1962-Present

廣西出生，著名龍虎武師。有一股狂莽氣勢，故常演歹角。十四歲加入武術隊，接受長達八年的武術訓練。後來因劉家良而進入戲行，參與與多部影畫戲的替身和演出工作。曾於《黃飛鴻》第一集負責李連杰的替身；第二集扮演邪教教主九宮真人；第三集戲份加碼，扮演黃飛鴻的徒弟鬼腳七。熊欣欣，鬼魅般的腿功技驚四座，名動江湖。後來因越來越多幕前演出機會，他亦從此有越來越多合作武俠影畫的機會，後來與徐克導演再度合作武俠影畫《刀》，扮演馬賊頭目，身手快如疾風，充滿邪氣，繼鬼腳七後再次演活一位武林高手。

熊欣欣

Born in Guangxi, Hung Yan Yan was known for his reckless temperament and tendency to play evil characters. At the age of 14, he joined a martial arts team and received eight years of formal martial arts training. Later, because of Lau Kar-Leung, Hung entered showbiz as a stand-in in many films. In the first Wong Fei-Hung film, he was Jet Li's stand-in; in the second film, he played the cult leader Jiugong Zhenren; and in the third film, he played the role of Wong Fei-Hung's apprentice, Kick Boxer. Hung Yan Yan's swift legwork shocked audiences and propelled him to fame. Afterwards, he was given many more opportunities and even collaborated with director Tsui Hark on the martial arts film "The Blade" (1995), playing a bloodthirsty bandit with superior fighting skills.

COLLIN CHOU
1967-Present

鄒兆龍的別名。

寶島武生。眼神兇狠、身形健碩，走兇惡型路線。十二歲便投身武行，並開始修練跆拳道與泰拳。在寶島服完兵役後往香港發展，加入了洪家班拜洪金寶為師，拍攝了多部動作戲。後來赴美進修，獲邀於西方科幻功夫片《廿二世紀殺人網絡》續集出演一角，於戲內表演真正的中國武術，躍向國際舞台。不過對香港人而言，鄒兆龍最具代表性的角色一直都是在以古諷今的古裝法庭戲《九品芝麻官》中的大奸角常威：一個陰險毒辣、誣衊無辜平民的富家子弟。由於他入木三分的演技，常威變相成為了鄒兆龍的別名。

鄒兆龍

A Formosa-born martial artist known for his hunky stature and vicious gaze, Collin Chou devoted himself to martial arts at the age of 12 and began to practice Taekwondo and Muay Thai. After serving in the military, he went to Hong Kong and worked under Sammo Hung. Later on, he went to the States to further his studies and was invited to act in "The Matrix Reloaded" (2003), where he performed Chinese martial arts and garnered international attention. However, for Hong Kongers, Collin's most representative role has always been the villain Chang Wei in "Hail the Judge" (1994), where locals still refer to him as Chang Wei due to his compelling performance.

LOUIS FAN
1973-Present

A Hong Kong-born martial artist known for his muscular body and thick eyebrows, Louis Fan was nicknamed the King of Power. He started training in martial arts at the age of 13 upon the encouragement of his father, Fan Mei-Sheng, who was also a famous martial artist. In fact, the elder Fan hired six masters to teach his son boxing and weapon-based Kung Fu. As a child, Louis often made cameo appearances in films and returned to acting in adulthood. In 1992, he starred in the film "Riki-Oh: The Story of Ricky", which was adapted from Japanese manga. With multiple shots of muscle-flexing, blood-spilling, and cheap stunts, the film was regarded as a cult movie by later generations. In 2008, Louis returned to the big screen and played the role of Shandong martial artist Kam Shan-Chau in "Ip Man", showing off his new image as a Northern hunk and becoming active on screen again.

香港出生的武生，肌肉發達、濃眉大眼，外號「力王」。十三歲開始習武。父親樊梅生是著名龍虎武師，曾聘請六名國術師傅教授兒子拳腳和兵器功夫。樊少皇兒時常於電影客串，長大後重返戲行，九二年憑東洋連環圖改篇的《力王》引發關注。他於戲內不單大展肌肉，打鬥場面亦大灑狗血，加上廉價特技，令該片被後世奉為邪典電影。零八年，於《葉問》一片扮演山東武師金山找，造型和氣質皆與過往角色不同，甚有北方大漢的粗野味道。他亦憑該片再次活躍於銀幕。

MAX ZHANG
1974-Present

Born in Chongqing, Max Zhang began to practice martial arts at the age of nine. He used to be a national martial arts athlete and has successively won competitions for the Chen Style Tai Chi Fist and Tai Chi Sword, on top of being the runner-up of the Eight Trigram Palm, Drunken Swordfighting, and pair training in the National Wushu Competition. After retiring from professional sports, he worked with the Yuens as a stand-in and a martial arts instructor, eventually making his way onto the big screen. With his sharp features and toned body, he mainly played villains in his early works. In 2013, he was the gloomy and reckless Shape-Will Fist master Ma San in "The Grandmaster".

生於重慶，九歲開始習武。眼尖、鼻尖、面尖，身形瘦削而結實，眼神有力，屬銳利型武生。曾是國家武英級武術運動員，先後取得全國武術比賽陳式太極拳和太極劍冠軍，槍術、劍術冠軍，及八卦掌、醉劍、對練亞軍，並於全運會獲得八卦掌、槍、劍金牌。退役後加入袁家班擔任替身和武術指導，之後開始幕前演出，早期作品以扮演反派為主。一三年於《一代宗師》扮演既陰沉又狂莽的形意拳高手馬三，因亮眼表現而名動江湖，亦因此獲得更多幕前表演機會。

First published and distributed by
viction:workshop ltd.

viction:ary™

viction:workshop ltd.
Unit C, 7/F, Seabright Plaza,
9-23 Shell Street, North Point, Hong Kong SAR

Url: victionary.com
Email: we@victionary.com
 @victionworkshop
 @victionworkshop
Bē @victionary
 @victionary

Edited and produced by viction:workshop ltd.
Book design by viction:workshop ltd.
Chinese text edited by Chiu Yan

©2023 viction:workshop ltd.

ISBN 978-988-74629-0-3
Printed and bound in China